STOP LETTING
EVERY
THING
AFFECT YOU

HOW TO BREAK FREE FROM OVERTHINKING, EMOTIONAL CHAOS, AND SELF-SABOTAGE

DANIEL CHIDIAC

UNDERCOVER
PUBLISHING HOUSE

Stop Letting Everything Affect You

Copyright © 2025 by Daniel Chidiac

First published by Undercover Publishing House Pty Ltd.

ISBN: 978-1-7641108-0-8

Printed in the United States of America

This book is dedicated to your growth.
-Daniel Chidiac

CONTENTS

PART 3

The Weight You Carry–
Boundaries And Detachment   81

PART 4

The Breaking Point–
Recognition and Realization   113

PART 5

Beyond the Surface – The Different Ideas That Are Just As Important

PART 6

Ways To Freedom

PART 7

The Light

STOP LETTING EVERYTHING AFFECT YOU

INTRODUCTION

There comes a moment when you realize you can't keep living like this—constantly drained, constantly affected by things that shouldn't have this much power over you. Maybe you've spent years feeling like you have no control over your own emotions, like every little thing—what someone says, what someone does, what doesn't go your way—dictates how you feel. Maybe you've been walking through life carrying invisible weights, things that were never even yours to hold.

You wake up already tense, already anticipating stress. You replay old conversations, dwell on things you can't change, and feel yourself being pulled into the same cycles—**overthinking, over-caring, overreacting**, and more times than you should be, spiralling out of control. Sometimes it's just a feeling that won't quite go away. An undercurrent of anxiety that neither takes full hold or fully disappears, but just lingers around enough to hold you hostage. Other times, it's so bad, all you want to do is run away. **You just want to run!** You literally think you're going crazy; that no "normal" person lets things affect them so easily, or so much. Even though it's hard to admit, you constantly find yourself being emotionally and mentally unstable. And you continue in this loop that just won't let up. You think you're all good again and you're on a high, and the next moment you feel like your world is crashing down around you. And deep down, you know it's not just about other people. It's not just about who hurt you, who let you down, who didn't appreciate you. **It's about you. It's about the way you've let everything and everyone have access to your peace, to your mind, to your emotions. It's about how hard you are on yourself.**

The cost of this emotional rollercoaster is immense. It affects your relationships, as people never know which version of you they'll encounter. It impacts your work, as your concentration fragments under the weight of internal chaos. It erodes your self-trust, as you question whether you can rely on yourself to remain stable. Most devastatingly, it robs you of presence—the ability to fully experience your life as it unfolds, rather than being trapped in mental projections of what might happen or ruminating on what already has.

You've tried different approaches. Perhaps you've attempted to suppress your emotions, only to have them burst forth later with even greater intensity. Maybe you've sought validation from others, hoping their reassurance would quiet the storm inside. Or you've tried to control every situation, believing that if you could just predict and manage every outcome, you'd finally feel at peace. But these strategies have failed you time and again, because they address symptoms rather than the root cause.

What you haven't yet realized is that this hyper-reactivity isn't a character flaw or some unchangeable aspect of your personality. It's a learned pattern, a habit of mind that has strengthened over time through repetition. And like any habit, it can be unlearned and replaced with healthier responses. The reactive mind isn't who you are—it's simply what you've practiced becoming.

But here's the truth: you don't have to live this way. You can change.

This journey won't always be easy. Growth isn't linear—it's a series of expansions and contractions, breakthroughs and setbacks. But with consistent practice and the tools provided in these pages, you'll develop a steadiness that remains unshaken, even when circumstances are chaotic.

This book is not about becoming emotionless. It's about learning to control what you give your energy to. It's about understanding that not everything deserves a reaction, not everyone deserves access to you, and not every thought is worth believing. It's about setting boundaries and protecting your peace—without guilt.

This book will teach you how to:

- Stop letting little things ruin your entire day.
- Stop self-sabotaging.
- Set healthy boundaries without feeling guilty.
- Recognize the difference between real guilt and manipulation.
- Break the cycle of overthinking before it spirals out of control.

- Stop taking everything so personally and free yourself from emotional reactivity.
- Identify toxic patterns in relationships and walk away without regret.
- Be more in control and feel better everyday.
- Shift your mindset from victimhood to self-empowerment.
- Learn the art of emotional detachment—how to be unbothered without becoming cold.
- Move forward unapologetically, without feeling the need to explain your growth.

Remember, you are not weak for feeling things deeply or overthinking, but you do have to stop letting those consume you. You are not selfish for choosing yourself, but you do have to stop apologizing for it. You are not heartless for walking away from what no longer serves you, but you do have to stop explaining yourself to people who will never understand.

This is your turning point. Let's begin uncovering why everything affects you so deeply—and then, how to finally break free...

PART 1

WHY YOU LET
EVERYTHING AFFECT YOU

CHAPTER 1

The Root of the Problem: Why You Feel Everything So Deeply

Have you ever wondered why certain things seem to affect you more than they do other people? Why a simple comment, a certain look, or even the tone in someone's voice can sit with you for hours, sometimes even days? Why your emotions can feel so strong that they completely take over, leaving you exhausted, overthinking, and overwhelmed? If so, you're not alone. Some people are just wired to feel things more deeply. It's not a weakness, and it's not something that makes you "too sensitive"—it's simply the way you experience the world. But when emotions feel like they have too much control over your life, it can start to feel like a curse.

For deeply feeling people, life isn't just something they go through—it's something they **absorb**. Every conversation, every interaction, every little moment is felt on a deeper level. This can be beautiful because it allows you to connect with people in meaningful ways, appreciate the small things, and experience emotions in a way that others may never fully understand. But it can also be exhausting. When you feel everything so deeply, the hard moments aren't just hard—they're **all-consuming**. A simple misunderstanding can feel like rejection. A small mistake can turn into a spiral of self-doubt. A passing comment from someone can stick with you long after they've forgotten they even said it.

The reason some people feel more intensely than others comes down to a mix of genetics, personality, and life experiences. Some people are naturally more in tune with emotions—they pick up on small details that others might miss, they notice shifts in tone or body language, and they process things in a way that makes experiences feel much bigger. Research on **Highly Sensitive People (HSPs)** by Dr. Elaine Aron (1997) suggests that about 20% of the population is born with a more reactive nervous system. This means their brains process sensory input and emotional cues more deeply than others. On top of that, childhood experiences play a big role. If you grew up in an environment where emotions weren't validated, you might have learned to overanalyze them as a way of making sense of things. If you grew up in a place where you had to be extra aware of people's moods, you may have developed a heightened sensitivity to everything around you.

The problem isn't just that you feel deeply—it's that you don't know how to turn it off. You don't just experience your own emotions strongly; you also absorb the emotions of others. You walk into a room and instantly sense the energy. If someone is upset, you feel it. If someone is acting differently, you notice. It's like carrying an emotional radar that's always on, always picking up signals, always processing. While this can make you empathetic and understanding, it can also leave you drained because you're carrying the weight of emotions that aren't even yours.

The problem with being empathetic is that you even feel sorry for people who hurt you.

This level of sensitivity also leads to **overthinking everything**. Your brain constantly replays conversations, searching for hidden meanings. You second-guess things you said, worried that you might have come across the wrong way. You assume that if someone is being quiet, it must have something to do with you. This overanalysis doesn't just keep your mind busy—it keeps you stuck. You get lost in cycles of self-doubt, worrying about things that don't actually matter as much as they feel like they do.

One of the biggest struggles for deeply feeling people is the sense of **guilt** that comes with it. You feel guilty for caring too much. You feel guilty for taking things too personally. You feel guilty for not being able to just "let things go" like everyone tells you to. And because you feel emotions so strongly, you might also feel responsible for how other people feel. You overextend yourself, you put others first, and you do everything you can to keep the peace—even when it comes at the expense of your own well-being.

19

The exhaustion that comes from feeling everything deeply isn't just mental—it's physical too. When your emotions are constantly heightened, your nervous system is always on high alert. Your body carries stress in ways you don't even realize. This is why some people who feel deeply also struggle with anxiety, tension, headaches, or even exhaustion from simply being around people. Your body isn't just reacting to your own emotions—it's reacting to the emotional weight of everything and everyone around you. But feeling everything so deeply doesn't just leave you emotionally exhausted—it can also make you care too much, stretching yourself thin in ways you don't even realize....

THE EMOTIONAL COST OF CARING TOO MUCH

Caring is supposed to be a good thing. It's what makes us human. It helps us connect, love, and build meaningful relationships. But what happens when caring becomes something that drains you instead of fulfilling you? When it starts to feel like an emotional weight you can't put down? When you care so much about everything—what people think, how they feel, what they need—that it leaves you feeling **empty, exhausted, and unappreciated**?

For those who care deeply, life often feels like a never-ending emotional investment. You put your heart into everything— your relationships, your friendships, even the smallest interactions with strangers. You give your time, your energy, and your emotions without hesitation. And yet, instead of feeling fulfilled, you often feel worn out, taken for granted, or even resentful. It's not that you don't want to care—it's that you don't know how to stop, even when it's hurting you.

Caring too much comes at a cost, and that cost is often **your own emotional well-being**. When you constantly put others first, there's little room left for yourself. Your own needs, feelings, and desires get pushed to the background. You tell yourself it's okay, that making others happy is worth it, but deep down, it's draining you. Over time, this imbalance leaves you feeling emotionally depleted, like you're constantly giving but never receiving.

One of the biggest struggles of caring too much is the weight of emotional responsibility. You feel responsible for making sure people are okay. You feel guilty if you can't fix their problems. You take on their emotions as if they're your own, and when they're struggling, it feels like your job to make it better. But the truth is, you can't save everyone. You can't carry the emotional burdens of the people around you and expect to stay emotionally intact yourself. No matter how much you care, **other people's happiness is not your responsibility**—and when you believe it is, you set yourself up for exhaustion and disappointment.

> *I used to think I could save everyone,*
> *until I realized they were drowning me.*

Another hidden cost of caring too much is how easily it can lead to overextending yourself. You say yes when you want to say no. You show up for people who wouldn't do the same for you. You push yourself beyond your limits because you don't want to let anyone down. But what happens when you keep pouring from an empty cup? You end up mentally drained, emotionally fragile, and sometimes even physically exhausted. And the worst part? Sometimes the people you bend over backward for don't even notice the sacrifices you're making.

Caring too much can also make you vulnerable to being taken advantage of. When people see that you'll always show up, always say yes, always care—some will start to expect it, not appreciate it. They'll assume you'll always be there, no matter how they treat you. And because you care so much, you'll tolerate things you shouldn't. You'll excuse behavior that hurts you. You'll stay in one-sided relationships, friendships, and situations that leave you feeling **unseen and unvalued**.

But here's the hard truth: **caring about people doesn't mean they'll care about you in the same way**. And that realization is painful. It's what leads to quiet resentment, burnout, and emotional exhaustion. It's what makes you feel drained by the very relationships you once cherished. When you care too much without limits, you end up carrying the emotional weight of everyone else while struggling to hold yourself together.

CHAPTER 2

The Problem Isn't Just People, It's Everything

HOW YOU LET LIFE OVERWHELM YOU

I remember a particular day when everything felt like too much. It wasn't anything catastrophic—just an ordinary morning that unraveled into something heavier than I could handle.

I woke up feeling exhausted even though I'd slept. My phone was the first thing I saw—notifications stacked on top of each other, reminders of things I hadn't done, messages I didn't have the energy to answer. I told myself I'd get to them later, but the guilt was already there, weighing me down before I even got out of bed. I rushed through my morning, already running behind. Then, I spilled my coffee. Not a big deal, right? But in that moment, it felt like the final straw. Like the universe was proving that no matter how hard I tried, I couldn't even get the simple things right.

I had to change my clothes, which made me even later, which made me even more anxious. By the time I got into my car, I was gripping the steering wheel so tightly my knuckles turned white. Every red light felt personal, every slow driver felt like they were intentionally in my way. My mind spiraled: *I should've left earlier. I should be more organized. Why can't I just get my life together?*

By the time I made it to my meeting, I wasn't just stressed—I was completely drained. I walked in, plastered on a neutral expression, and pretended everything was fine. But inside, I felt like I was drowning in things I couldn't even name. **That's the thing about overwhelm—it doesn't hit all at once. It creeps up on you**, disguised as small, insignificant moments. It's the weight of expectations—your own, other people's, society's—all pressing down until you feel like you can't breathe.

You tell yourself you should be able to handle it. Other people seem to manage just fine. So why does life always feel like too much? **The truth is, it's not just one thing—it's everything.** Your day isn't made up of big crises but of dozens of small moments that each demand something from you. Each notification, each task, each interaction requires energy. And when your resources are already depleted, even the smallest request can feel monumental.

Think about it—have you ever had a day where something went wrong, but it didn't really bother you? Maybe you laughed it off and moved on. And then other days, something just as small sets you off completely. **The difference isn't the situation itself; it's your mental state when it happens.**

If you don't process your emotions as they come, they don't just disappear—they pile up in the background. When you don't have an outlet for them, they look for any excuse to surface. That's why you might end up crying over something as trivial as dropping your phone—because it's not just about the phone. **It's about everything else you've been holding in.**

Psychologist John Sweller's Cognitive Load Theory (1998) explains why even small stressors can feel unbearable when your brain is already overloaded. Your brain has a limited capacity for processing information at any given moment. When too much stress or decision-making is competing for mental space, your brain struggles to function efficiently.

Imagine your mind like your bedroom. When your room is messy—clothes scattered everywhere, piles of laundry, random objects covering every surface—it feels overwhelming. You might put up with it for days, some people even weeks. You notice it, you acknowledge that it's slightly bothering you, but you let it go. And then one day, walking into that same room makes you tense because it's chaotic, and finding what you need takes extra effort. You're not just dealing with the task at hand; your brain is now also subconsciously processing all the visual clutter.

Now, think about how it feels when your room is clean—everything in its place, open space, nothing extra demanding your attention. Suddenly, the room feels bigger. You can breathe easier, relax more, and focus better. **Your brain works the same way.** When your mental space is cluttered with stress, decisions, and unfinished thoughts, even the smallest inconvenience feels overwhelming. Not because it's a big deal, but because your brain is already at capacity.

And when our brain is at capacity, it often causes emotional reactions that are connected to deeper wounds. Our outward reactions may seem disproportionate because they're not just about the present moment—they're about every similar experience we've ever had. Getting cut off in traffic might not seem like a big deal, but in that moment, it can feel like proof that people are selfish and inconsiderate. Someone not replying to your text right away might feel like rejection, even though it's probably not. These reactions aren't always logical, but they're being driven by underlying beliefs and emotional wounds that haven't fully healed.

What can make gaining control over our mind and life even harder, is the world we live in today. We're constantly bombarded with information, comparisons, and pressure to keep up. Social media shows us people who seem to be doing more, achieving more, living better. Work expects us to be available at all times. Society convinces us that if we're not constantly improving, we're failing. It's no wonder so many of us feel like we're on the verge of burnout.

The problem isn't just that people drain you or that your thoughts overwhelm you—it's that life itself has become

an endless series of inputs, expectations, and demands that few of us were ever taught how to manage. And when our minds are overwhelmed by this constant input overload, they don't simply shut down—they go into overdrive. This is where the real prison begins to form: in how our minds process, ruminate on, and amplify these pressures until they consume us.

CHAPTER 3

The Thought Prison: How Your Mind Creates Mental Loops

Often, your mind plays tricks on you. And it's because of these tricks that we get caught-up in overthinking. This is where it gets interesting... Subconsciously, it tries to convince you that if you think about something long enough, you'll somehow gain control over it. At first, you might convince yourself it's helping—that by analyzing every detail, you're preventing mistakes or protecting yourself from pain. But what you don't realize is that overthinking isn't protecting you. **It's trapping you in a cycle psychologists call the "anxiety loop".**

This loop begins when your brain fixates on a worry, feeds it with more stress, and then convinces you that you must keep thinking about it to "solve" it. But the more you engage, the worse it gets. *It's like quicksand—the harder you struggle, the deeper you sink.*

The worst part? **Most of the things you're anxious about never even happen**. I'm sure you're all too familiar with how your mind replays conversations, analyzes what you should have said, and imagines worst-case scenarios that haven't even happened. You lose sleep over scenarios that never play out. You rehearse arguments that never take place. You brace yourself for disappointment that never comes. And even if something does go wrong, it's rarely as bad as your mind made it out to be. Yet your brain keeps running the same cycle again and again.

Consider what happens when someone doesn't text you back right away. Your brain doesn't think, *Oh, they're probably busy*. Instead, it jumps to: *Did I say something wrong? Are they mad at me? Are they losing interest?* If a friend seems distant, instead of assuming they might be having a bad day, your mind immediately goes to: *They must be upset with me. Did I do something? What if they don't want me in their life anymore?*

Your brain doesn't like uncertainty, so it creates a narrative—one that usually leans toward negativity. These aren't occasional thoughts; they become **core beliefs that shape how you see yourself and the world**.

Your brain is wired to focus on threats—a survival mechanism that once protected our ancestors from danger. Psychologists often refer to this as the **negativity bias**: your brain naturally fixates on negative experiences more than positive ones, even when there's no real threat. Research by Baumeister and colleagues (2001) demonstrated that negative events have a greater impact on our psychological state than positive ones of equal intensity. This hypervigilance kept our ancestors alive, but in modern life, your brain isn't warning you about actual danger—it's warning you about embarrassment, rejection, failure, and uncertainty.

Your brain craves certainty. It wants answers. It wants to predict outcomes. It wants to prepare for every possible worst-case scenario, because in some twisted way, it believes that if it worries enough, it can prevent bad things from happening or find the right decision to make. This is an illusion—**worrying doesn't prevent anything, and rarely decides the right decision, it just steals your peace in the present moment.** Research on decision fatigue by Baumeister and colleagues (1998) revealed that the more mental energy you spend on unnecessary worries, the less capable you are of making clear, rational decisions. Anxiety drains your ability to focus, leaving you mentally exhausted but no closer to a solution.

WHY YOUR MIND CLINGS TO PAIN

Overthinking isn't just about survival—it's also about emotional pain. At some point, you learned that pain demands attention. Maybe it was a past mistake that still haunts you, or a relationship that left you broken. Maybe you grew up in an environment where you constantly had to be on edge, preparing for the next disappointment. Whatever the reason, your brain got used to holding onto pain instead of letting it go.

Here's the hard truth: **pain can become familiar—so familiar that you don't even realize you're clinging to it**. When you've been hurt, your brain wants to keep replaying it, as if going over it enough times will change what happened. But instead of finding closure, you just keep reopening the wound. *It's like scratching at a cut instead of letting it heal.*

This is why some people unconsciously seek out situations that reinforce their pain. They chase after unavailable people, stay in toxic cycles, or put themselves in positions where they'll be disappointed. Not because they enjoy suffering, but because it's what they know. If your mind has been conditioned to expect pain, then peace can feel unfamiliar—even uncomfortable. Without even realizing it, you keep going back to what hurts you, simply because it feels normal. And, it's usually overthinking that disguises these habits. For example, when something feels peaceful in our life, our brain will go into overdrive of what could potentially go wrong. And if we don't know how to handle that situation when it arises and allow it to take root, it can subconsciously cause us to self-sabotage. Then, back we go into the chaos.

Psychologist Susan Nolen-Hoeksema (2000) conducted groundbreaking research on rumination—the act of continuously thinking about distressing experiences. Her studies found that rumination actually feeds into anxiety and depression rather than resolving them. **The more you replay past pain, the harder it becomes to break free from it**. Instead of helping you process emotions, overthinking deepens your emotional suffering, making it even more difficult to move on.

Realizing you grew up too young, fell in love too young, dealt with the hardest battles too young, and now you're an overstimulated adult who has been in fight or flight mode most their life and trying to be the best version of yourself.

Your thoughts don't just influence how you feel—they shape your entire reality. The stories your mind tells become the lens through which you see everything. And because these stories come from inside your own head, you assume they must be true. You don't even question them. But here's the fundamental truth you need to understand: **your thoughts are not reality**. Your brain is not a perfect machine that only delivers facts. It is shaped by your fears, insecurities, and past experiences. It jumps to conclusions. It fills in gaps. It creates problems that don't exist.

When something feels unclear or unknown, your brain tries to fill in the gaps—and often, it does this by assuming the worst. This doesn't mean it's reality. **Most times, you're seeing things worse than they actually are, not how they really are.** In the grand scheme of things, most of the things we overreact about aren't that serious. They definitely aren't serious enough to justify a meltdown or going into fight-or-flight mode.

These mental narratives become automatic over time. You don't even realize you're telling yourself the same things every day. It just feels like reality. But these stories are just perspectives you've accepted—not facts.

*If you believe you're not enough, you'll replay moments where you felt overlooked while ignoring **times you were valued**. If you believe people always leave, you'll focus on every time someone walked away while ignoring **the people who stayed**.* Your brain isn't looking for the truth—it's looking for proof of the stories you've already decided to believe.

WHY THESE PATTERNS PERSIST

There are several reasons why these mental loops persist:

1. **Your brain rewards overthinking**, even when it doesn't help you. Every time you engage with anxious thoughts, you reinforce neural pathways that make those thoughts more accessible in the future. Your brain essentially becomes more efficient at producing the thoughts you engage with most frequently.

2. **Your brain prefers familiarity**. Even if a belief is painful, it's comfortable because it's what you know. Changing it feels uncomfortable because it challenges the version of reality you've held onto for so long. This is called "cognitive consistency"—the tendency to maintain beliefs even when evidence contradicts them.

3. **You've never actively challenged these thoughts**. You've accepted them as part of who you are rather than questioning their validity. Cognitive behavioral therapy (CBT), one of the most evidence-based

33

approaches to treating anxiety, focuses specifically on identifying and challenging these automatic thoughts.

4. **Letting go feels irresponsible**. Your brain convinces you that if you stop thinking about something, you're being careless. But letting go doesn't mean ignoring your problems—it means accepting what you can't control. Research on mindfulness shows that observing thoughts without attaching to them actually leads to better problem-solving.

The more you dwell on negative thoughts, the deeper they become ingrained in your mind, making it harder to break the cycle. Nolen-Hoeksema's research demonstrated that people who ruminate recover more slowly from depression and are more likely to develop it in the first place.

One single thought can snowball into a full-blown crisis—all because your brain assumes that every thought it produces must be taken seriously. Maybe you make a small mistake at work, and before you know it, your thoughts have convinced you that you're terrible at your job and that failure is inevitable. Maybe you wake up feeling a little anxious, and instead of letting the feeling pass, your brain latches onto it: *What if something is seriously wrong with me? What if I feel like this forever?*

Over time, you don't just think about pain—**you start identifying with it**. You mistake your thoughts for reality, your fears for truth. But your thoughts are not you, and they are not necessarily true. They are just thoughts. And the moment you stop treating them as absolute truth, you give yourself the freedom to finally let go.

Understanding these patterns is the first step toward recognizing their power over you. When you see that your thoughts are creating these loops—not external reality—you begin to realize how much influence they have. **The prison exists only in your mind.**

This is where stepping back becomes not just helpful, but essential. When we're caught in these mental loops, we're seeing everything through a keyhole—a narrow, distorted view that magnifies our problems and minimizes our resilience. To break free, we need to widen our perspective dramatically—not just beyond our immediate thoughts, but beyond our human-sized concerns altogether.

CHAPTER 4

The Bigger Perspective

Imagine stepping outside of your own mind for a moment. Picture an observer from another planet, watching Earth from a distance. They're looking at the mountains, the oceans, the vibrant ecosystems teeming with life. They see people waking up every day, surrounded by endless opportunities to experience, to love, to create, to simply exist in this miraculous reality. And they know they are only given one life to experience it. Then, they look around at their own planet, and it's lifeless. Nothing but a ball of dust. No life, like an empty vessel.

When I think about this scenario, it makes me truly wonder what someone else would think of us looking down. From this cosmic viewpoint, it's almost laughable, but it's not. It's just sad. The universe, vast and indifferent, stretches endlessly in every direction, and here we are—on this tiny, breathtakingly beautiful planet—obsessing over whether someone liked our social media post, whether we said something embarrassing at dinner last night, or whether we're measuring up to societal expectations. We are literally wasting our lives stressing on the most beautiful planet that we know of. Think about it. Every time we are stressing, we are wasting precious time, and for what? We live as if we have infinite time, as if we can afford to waste days, weeks, or even years trapped in mental loops of worry and fear.

How many family gatherings, how many events or experiences have been tarnished by being affected by someone else's actions toward you? How many times have you been somewhere but your mind has been somewhere else? Spending time with loved ones but not being truly present. So many previous memories and moments wasted. And for what? Caring or worrying over what? The truth is, our time here is limited. We are all going to die!

One day you won't be here to do any of the things you love. In fact, you won't even have to wait until death. At a certain age (if some of us get there), you physically won't be able to do them. You will be too old and physically unable to walk around freely on your own, let alone jump in the ocean, meet new people, or explore this beautiful world. A lot of the people who you love today, will be gone. And what will you look back and say? *"It was good that I stressed for two months about the person who didn't text me back"*? I promise you will look back with regret. It's not about dismissing the issues we face, but about putting into perspective the magnitude we give them.

> *This year instead of worrying about what's under the tree, maybe just be grateful for who's still here to be around it.*

Stepping back and seeing life from a higher perspective allows us to regain clarity. Think of it like looking at your hand. When it's pressed against the tip of your nose, you can't see it clearly. Now move it away and look. It's the same with our problems, and with life. Sometimes we cannot solve the problem by constantly thinking about it. We need distance. We need space to see the whole picture. The next time you catch yourself spiraling, try to zoom out. Ask yourself, *"Will this matter or have as much power in three months, six months or a year from now?"* And be honest with yourself about the answer. More often than not, the answer is no. Sometimes it might not matter in a couple of weeks.

A big part of the reason we worry and stress is because we don't see the whole picture. Some of us also love the concept of thinking we are always in control. Consider the profound story of Job in the Bible—one of history's most powerful examples of human suffering and meaning. Whether you're religious or not, Job's story reflects our shared humanity during times of suffering and powerlessness. At its core, it teaches us about **letting go and accepting that we can't always understand why things happen the way they do, when they do.** Here was a man who lost everything: his children, his wealth, his health, everything he'd built and everyone he loved. In the midst of this unimaginable suffering, Job cries out for answers. He demands to know why he, a man who he believes has a good heart, should suffer so terribly. And what's fascinating about this ancient story is God's response.

When God finally speaks, He doesn't actually answer Job's individual questions directly. He doesn't explain why the suffering happened or offer comfort in the way Job expects in that moment. Instead, God responds with questions of His own: **"Where were you when I laid the foundation of the earth? Tell me, if you have understanding. Who determined its measurements—surely you know!"** God takes Job on a cosmic tour, showing him the vast complexity of creation, from the patterns of stars to the birth of mountain goats. The message is clear and humbling: Job's perspective is painfully limited. From his human vantage point, suffering seems senseless and cruel. But there's a larger pattern at work that he cannot possibly comprehend. This also seconds one of Job's friends advice. Unlike three of his other friends (Eliphaz, Bildad and Zophar), who argue that Job's suffering must be due to his sins, Elihu argues that the reason for suffering can also be for spiritual growth and purification.

This isn't to dismiss the intensity of suffering at times. Rather, it's a powerful reminder of how limited our view can be. We see only a tiny fragment of the pattern—a few threads in an immense tapestry. That's why we have to learn to let go and trust that there may be purpose and meaning even in experiences that seem senseless from our perspective. And we know this is possible because of those moments in our own lives when what initially seemed like disaster, later revealed itself as necessary transformation. Those moments we never thought we'd get out of, that later proved to be the very experiences that shaped us into who we needed to become.

When you're caught in stress or anxiety, pause. Take a breath. Remember that your perspective is limited right now. The thing that's consuming your thoughts is probably not as significant as it feels. And even if it is challenging, remember how much else there is in this vast universe that's working perfectly, beautifully, exactly as it should. With this broader perspective in mind, you're now ready to explore practical techniques that can help you break free from the mental and emotional patterns that keep you trapped. These aren't just temporary fixes—they're transformative practices that will gradually change how you relate to your thoughts, emotions, and the world around you.

PART 1

Solutions

THE WITNESS PRACTICE:
TRANSFORMING YOUR RELATIONSHIP
WITH EMOTIONS

At the heart of emotional freedom lies a simple but profound shift: learning to witness your emotions rather than becoming them. When you're caught in intense feelings, you lose perspective. You are no longer you—you are the anger, the anxiety, the hurt. This complete identification with emotions is what makes them so overwhelming.

The Witness Practice breaks this pattern through three connected steps:

First, name what you're experiencing specifically. This isn't just a mental exercise—it's neurological alchemy. When you label an emotion precisely ("I'm feeling disappointed" rather than "I feel bad"), you activate your prefrontal cortex, the rational part of your brain that can modulate emotional intensity. Brain imaging studies show that this simple act of naming reduces activity in the amygdala, your emotional alarm system.

Next, create linguistic distance. Instead of saying "I am angry," try "I notice anger arising in me right now." This subtle shift positions you as the observer of your emotions rather than being identical to them. You're acknowledging the emotion without letting it define you completely. This isn't denying how you feel—it's recognizing that you are larger than any feeling passing through you.

Finally, bring awareness to the physical sensations. Where do you feel this emotion in your body? Is there tightness in your chest? A knot in your stomach? Heat in your face? By anchoring your attention in physical sensations, you pull yourself out of the mental stories that intensify emotions and ground yourself in direct experience. This embodied awareness turns abstract emotional suffering into manageable physical experience.

Practice this sequence daily, especially with smaller emotions, so it becomes second nature when stronger feelings arise. The more you practice witnessing your emotions rather than becoming them, the more space you create—and in that space lies your freedom.

THE ATTENTION RESTORATION SYSTEM: CREATING MENTAL SPACE

*Sometimes you can literally be fighting for your
life and people will only notice that you aren't
showing up for them the way they want.*

The modern world wasn't designed for the sensitive nervous system. Every notification, conversation, and decision requires mental energy, and for deeply feeling people, this cognitive load can quickly become overwhelming. The key to sanity isn't just better time management—it's deliberate attention restoration.

Creating "attention sanctuaries" is essential for mental recovery. These are physical or temporal spaces completely free from demands on your attention. Unlike quick breaks that often involve different forms of stimulation (like checking social media), true attention sanctuaries allow your directed attention system—the neural network responsible for focus and emotional regulation—to genuinely reset.

Design your attention sanctuary with these elements:

Sensory simplicity: Choose an environment with minimal sensory input—a quiet corner, a peaceful outdoor space, or even a bathroom with the door locked if options are limited. Reduce visual clutter, noise, and other stimulation.

Technology absence: Keep your sanctuary completely device-free. No phones, computers, tablets, or watches that connect you to the digital world. This isn't just about avoiding distractions—it's about giving your brain a complete break from the cognitive load of connectivity.

Natural elements: Research shows that natural environments are particularly effective for attention restoration. Even small doses of nature—a view of trees, the sound of water, or holding a plant—can facilitate recovery.

Temporal boundaries: Decide in advance how long you'll spend in your sanctuary—even five minutes can be restorative if it's complete. Set a timer outside your sanctuary so you're not checking the time.

Schedule these attention restoration periods proactively throughout your day—ideally before you feel overwhelmed, not after. Even brief periods of complete attentional rest can prevent the cognitive depletion that leads to emotional reactivity and mental exhaustion.

This isn't indulgence—it's necessary maintenance for your most precious resource: your capacity for focused attention and emotional regulation. Research consistently shows that these brief restoration periods actually increase productivity and creativity while reducing stress hormones and reactive behavior.

THE THOUGHT CONTAINMENT PRACTICE: BREAKING FREE FROM RUMINATION

The Thought Containment Practice works by giving your brain what it's actually seeking when it ruminates: a sense of control and completion. Instead of trying to stop thoughts (which paradoxically makes them stronger), you're creating a structured container for them.

Here's how to implement it:

First, designate a specific "worry time" each day—15-20 minutes when you'll deliberately engage with your concerns. Choose a time when you typically have mental energy, not right before bed.

When intrusive thoughts arise outside this time, acknowledge them briefly with, "I see you, and I'll give you my full attention during worry time." Then write the thought in a dedicated notebook or digital note. This physical act of recording satisfies your brain's need to "hold onto" the concern without letting it consume your current moment.

During your designated worry time, review what you've written and give each concern your full attention. For each worry, ask yourself:

- Is there an action I can take about this now?
- If yes, what's the smallest first step?
- If no, can I accept this uncertainty for now?

After worry time ends, close your notebook or file, signaling to your brain that this session is complete. If the same thoughts return before your next worry time, remind yourself, "I've already captured this. I'll think about it during worry time."

This practice works because it honors your brain's need to process concerns while preventing them from infiltrating every moment of your day. Over time, your mind learns that these thoughts will get attention, just not immediately. This breaks the habit of instant rumination while still addressing legitimate concerns.

The key is consistency. At first, your brain will resist this structured approach, pushing you to engage with thoughts immediately. With practice, you'll find that urgent-feeling thoughts can usually wait, and many concerns that seemed pressing lose their intensity when deliberately examined during worry time.

For longstanding thought patterns that are deeply ingrained, pair this practice with a counter-narrative journal. Each day, write evidence that contradicts your negative beliefs, gradually building a case for a new perspective. What we focus on expands—by deliberately attending to evidence that challenges negative thought patterns, you begin rewriting the neural pathways that maintain them.

MENTAL STRENGTH CONDITIONING: BREAKING FREE FROM THOUGHT LOOPS

Research from Stanford University's neuroscience department has revealed something fascinating: the more you try to directly suppress unwanted thoughts, the more persistent they become (Wegner et al., 2012). It's like telling yourself "don't think about a white bear"—suddenly, white bears are everywhere in your mind. This "ironic processing" effect explains why traditional approaches like "just think positive" or "stop overthinking" actually backfire.

So how do you break free from these mental loops? The science points to two particularly effective approaches that work directly with your brain's architecture rather than against it.

The Thought Diffusion Exercise

When you're caught in a thought loop, try this technique that's been validated through multiple clinical studies at Harvard's psychology department:

1. Notice when you're stuck in a repetitive thought
2. Say to yourself: "I am noticing that I'm having the thought that..." followed by the specific thought
3. Then visualize the thought as text scrolling across a screen or written on leaves floating down a stream
4. Observe the thought passing by without engaging with its content

This creates psychological distance between you and your thoughts. Research by Masuda and colleagues (2010) demonstrated that this simple practice reduced both the emotional impact and believability of negative thoughts by over 40% compared to control groups who tried to suppress or argue with their thoughts.

The Pattern Interrupt + Pivot

Breaking thought loops requires both interrupting the current pattern and redirecting neural activity. Dr. Jeffrey Schwartz at UCLA School of Medicine developed this four-step approach that's proven effective even for severe thought patterns in OCD:

1. RELABEL: Identify the thought loop by name: "This is rumination" or "This is catastrophizing"
2. REATTRIBUTE: Remind yourself "This is my brain getting stuck, not an accurate reflection of reality"
3. REFOCUS: Immediately engage in a pre-selected absorbing activity that requires full attention (solving a math problem, naming everything blue in your environment, counting backward from 100 by 7s)
4. REVALUE: Afterward, briefly reflect: "That thought pattern isn't helpful or necessary"

Schwartz's research, published in the Archives of General Psychiatry, showed this technique actually changes brain activity patterns in the caudate nucleus—a key area involved in thought loops—when practiced consistently.

The key to both techniques is consistency. Like building any skill, breaking entrenched thought patterns takes practice. But neuroscience confirms that with repetition, these new responses become your brain's default setting. The thoughts may still arise—that's just your brain doing its job—but they no longer trap you in endless loops of rumination.

THE INTEGRATION: DAILY PRACTICE FOR LASTING CHANGE

These practices aren't separate techniques to try occasionally—they form an integrated system that, when practiced consistently, creates profound transformation over time. The key is implementation—knowing what to do isn't the same as doing it regularly enough to create change.

To integrate these practices into your daily life, create "implementation intentions"—specific plans for when and where you'll practice each technique. Research shows that these concrete plans make you far more likely to follow through than general intentions.

Morning: Begin with a brief Witness Practice. As you notice your first emotional responses of the day, practice naming, distancing, and embodying them. This sets the tone for conscious emotional awareness throughout the day.

Throughout the day: When emotions arise intensely, implement the Witness Practice. When intrusive thoughts begin spiraling, use the Thought Containment approach to record them for later consideration.

Midday: Schedule a 5-10 minute Attention Restoration period, completely disconnecting from demands and allowing your directed attention system to reset. Even this brief period can significantly reduce afternoon reactivity.

Evening: Review your thought container notebook during a designated worry time, addressing concerns systematically rather than randomly throughout the day. Before sleep, practice a brief gratitude reflection to counter the brain's negativity bias. *What is something good that happened today?* It may be small in your eyes or something that we usually take for granted, but acknowledging this is very important. Think hard if you have to...and you'll find multiple things that were good.

Remember that transformation isn't linear. There will be days when you forget these practices entirely, when emotions overwhelm you despite your best intentions, when thoughts spiral beyond your ability to contain them. This isn't failure—it's part of the process.

The goal isn't perfection but progress—gradually developing a new relationship with your emotions, your attention, and your thoughts. With consistent practice, what begins as conscious effort slowly becomes your natural way of being. The sensitivity that once felt like your greatest vulnerability becomes your greatest strength—allowing you to experience life's richness without being consumed by it.

This journey begins now, with your next breath, your next emotion, your next thought—and the awareness with which you meet it.

Diagram for quick interruption

Draw this out or take a photo and save it to your phone notes as "anxiety loop". The next time you are experiencing an **anxiety loop** of thoughts, look at it and follow it. Awareness and **action** are key to disrupt the pattern. Once you start having the Thoughts, you must Intervene. And you can intervene with a simple question: *How are thinking these thoughts, benefiting my life in any way?*

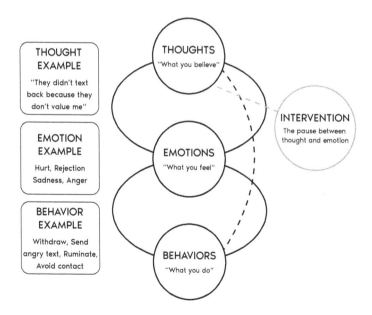

As you integrate these practices into your daily life, you'll begin to experience moments of clarity and calm. You'll notice spaces opening up between your emotions and your reactions to them. But what if there was an even more powerful approach—one that seems almost too simple? What if, instead of managing or containing difficult thoughts and feelings, you could completely transform your relationship with them through one surprisingly counterintuitive shift? This next technique builds on everything you've learned so far but works from an entirely different angle—one that might just change everything...

THE MOST RIDICULOUSLY EFFECTIVE WAY THAT CAN BEAT OVERTHINKING, ANXIETY AND SELF-SABOTAGE

Beyond the practices we've explored, there's another powerful approach to addressing overthinking and anxiety—one that seems so counterintuitive it might make you skeptical at first. This technique works alongside the other methods but tackles the problem from an entirely different angle. *"What you resist persists,"* wrote Carl Jung, highlighting a fundamental truth about the human mind. When we try to force unwanted thoughts away, we inadvertently strengthen them. Each attempt to suppress a thought becomes another reminder of exactly what you're trying to forget. This creates a double-bind: first you spiral about the original thought, then you spiral about trying not to think about it.

This additional tool may sound strange at first: **Say thank you to your anxiety.** Yes, it might sound ridiculous initially—thanking the very thing causing your distress? But this seemingly small shift holds tremendous potential. When anxiety strikes, simply smile and say, *"Thank you for this feeling. I appreciate this shift in energy. I love you."* For example, imagine that familiar moment when you replay a casual conversation from earlier in the day, fixating on something minor you said. "Did I come across as rude? Why did I phrase it that way? They must think I'm so awkward." Or when you post something on social media and think you've made a mistake. Whatever it is, instead of fighting these thoughts or trying to rationalize them away, you might say, "Thank you, anxiety, for showing up again...I've missed you." And do your best to feel the emotions, say the words out loud, or act out the expressions of being genuinely grateful.

Thanking the feeling creates an immediate shift in your relationship to it and loosening its grip without fighting it directly. This approach might seem too simple to work, but the science supports it. Research from UC Berkeley found that gratitude practices actively counteract negative emotions by triggering positive neural circuitry, effectively short-circuiting anxiety-producing thought patterns. Gratitude practices work by activating different neural networks than those involved in stress and anxiety.

Many people initially react with skepticism. *"How could thanking my anxiety possibly help when I've tried everything else?"* This skepticism is natural—our logical minds want to solve problems through analysis. But therein lies the paradox: your analytical mind—the very thing that created the spiral—cannot solve the problem it generated. This technique works precisely because it sidesteps analysis altogether. The effectiveness comes from combining verbal expression with physical and emotional alignment. As you express gratitude, allow yourself to smile—even smirk if that feels more natural. **This multi-sensory approach engages your entire system**, creating a powerful intervention.

Have you noticed that anxiety eventually dissipates not because you solved anything, but because you simply got distracted? Most of the time, the "problem" wasn't even real—it was a mental creation that dissolved when your attention shifted. So why not thank these feelings? This approach can work in harmony with the other techniques you've learned. Use the Witness Practice to create initial awareness, the Thought Containment method for persistent worries, and try this gratitude approach as an in-the-moment intervention when you feel yourself spiraling. Each tool has its place in your emotional regulation toolkit.

I've even started saying thank you when something seemingly negative happens. Many times in my life, what initially seemed bad actually worked in my favor. **Saying thank you during difficult moments lessens their power over me** and strengthens my faith in the unknown—believing everything is happening for me, not to me. It creates space and, paradoxically, gives me more control. Of course, there are genuinely difficult life events that we may not immediately feel thankful for. But starting with smaller daily frustrations is powerful. This isn't about forced positivity—it's about using your intelligence to connect with your inner power.

This approach embodies a profound paradox: **by embracing what troubles us, we diminish its power**. It's counterintuitive, which is precisely why it works when logical methods fail. Now that you have powerful tools for transforming your relationship with anxiety from within, it's time to address your relationship with the external world. While the "Thank You" practice helps you change internal responses, many of us still find ourselves at the mercy of external circumstances. The next section explores how we inadvertently give our power away to situations beyond our control and how to reclaim that power without trying to control the uncontrollable.

PART 2

YOU'RE LETTING LIFE CONTROL YOU

CHAPTER 5

The Illusion of Control

I'm at this stage of my life,
if I start catching bad vibes... I'm out.

One of the main reasons why small things stress you out so much is because they **break the illusion of control**. You try to keep your life in order, stay on top of things, plan your day a certain way—and then something as simple as dropping your phone completely throws you off. It's not really about dropping the phone. **It's about the fact that life didn't go the way you expected, and that makes you feel out of control.**

At its core, stress isn't just about what happens to you—it's about how much control you feel you have over it. When life doesn't go as planned, even in the smallest ways, your brain perceives it as a threat, not because the event itself is dangerous, but because it disrupts your expectations. And when you feel like things are spiraling beyond your control, your stress response goes into overdrive.

This is backed by research on **perceived control**—a psychological concept that refers to how much influence we believe we have over our environment and experiences. Studies have shown that people who feel a greater sense of control over **their lives**, experience **lower stress levels, better emotional regulation, and even improved physical health.** In contrast, those who feel like life is constantly happening *to* them, rather than being something they can actively shape, are more likely to experience chronic stress, anxiety, and even depression (Langer & Rodin, 1976).

One famous study on this was conducted in the **1970s in a nursing home by Ellen Langer and Judith Rodin.** In the study, one group of elderly residents was given control over small decisions in their daily lives—like choosing their own plants to care for, deciding what movies to watch, and scheduling their own social activities. The other group had everything chosen for them, with no real autonomy. The results? The residents who had more control **lived longer, were happier, and had significantly better health outcomes** compared to those who had little control.

This experiment demonstrates something critical: **even small feelings of control can make a big difference in how we handle stress.** And the same applies to how we deal with daily inconveniences. If you constantly feel like life is just throwing problems at you, you're going to feel exhausted and reactive. But if you shift your mindset and focus on the things you *can* control, your entire experience of stress changes.

So, feeling in control by its very nature can improve our lives, however it's the type of control we seek that is the determining factor. Here's the truth: you can't control everything. You can't control traffic, how other people act, or whether your day unfolds exactly as planned. But you *can* control how you interpret situations, how you react, and where you place your energy. Psychologist **Julian Rotter's concept of Locus of Control (1954)** explains this well. People with an **internal locus of control** believe that their actions shape their lives—including their ability to redirect their emotional responses—while those with an **external locus of control** feel like life is dictated by external forces—luck, fate, or other people. Research has shown that individuals with an **internal locus of control tend to be happier, more resilient, and better at handling stress** (Deci & Ryan, 1985). I found this to be very true in my own life. But also, as I went deeper into my own experiences, I discovered that control, rejection and the desire to "win" are actually all connected...

CHAPTER 6

The Connection between Control, Rejection and the Desire to "Win"

*When the person you loved the hardest
did you the dirtiest, it changes you.*

Wanting to always control the narratives in our mind is deeply connected to social rejection, which activates the **same neural pathways as physical pain** (Eisenberger, Lieberman & Williams, 2003). When people experience rejection, the dorsal anterior cingulate cortex (dACC) and anterior insula—the same brain regions that process physical pain—light up. This is why rejection feels so real and painful; the brain perceives it as a **threat to survival**, just like physical harm. From an evolutionary perspective, rejection used to mean being cast out from the tribe, which was essentially a death sentence in early human history. Our ancestors depended on group inclusion for protection, food, and survival. As a result, the brain evolved to desperately avoid rejection, making even small moments of uncertainty—like delayed responses or distant behavior—feel like they hold enormous weight.

It's important to realize that rejection isn't always about a romantic partner. It could be from a parent who was emotionally distant, a friend who abandoned you, a workplace that undervalued you, or even a childhood experience where you felt ignored, unwanted, or unworthy. The brain doesn't distinguish between types of rejection—it stores the emotional pain just the same. If you've been rejected, criticized, or blindsided before, your brain remembers it. And now, any small sign of uncertainty feels like it could be leading to that same kind of pain again. The brain despises feeling powerless, so when something is out of your hands, your instinct is to try to regain control. This is where control-seeking behaviors come into play. If a person feels powerless due to rejection, they might:

- Overanalyze the situation, searching for ways they could have changed the outcome.
- Obsess over proving themselves to the person or group that rejected them.
- Engage in self-blame, thinking if they just "did better," they would have prevented the rejection.

> When we look deeper, we find that sometimes we aren't really angry at them, but more angry at ourselves for allowing them to treat us that way.

This lack of control over how others perceive them creates intense emotional distress, leading people to seek control, or "let go" in other ways—through overthinking, perfectionism, self-sabotage through substance or alcohol abuse, or obsessing over how to "fix" the situation. The brain's craving for control doesn't stop at overthinking. It extends into the need to prove oneself—the desire to **"win"** in some way after experiencing rejection or uncertainty. When we achieve a goal, win an argument, or gain someone's approval, our brain releases dopamine, the neurotransmitter associated with pleasure, motivation, and reward (Tricomi, Rangel, Camerer & O'Doherty, 2010). This is the same system that fuels addictive behaviors—because success, validation, and even revenge give us a powerful dopamine hit.

This is why some people become obsessed with proving themselves after rejection. It's not just about resolving the emotional wound—it's about triggering the brain's reward system. Winning or seeking validation restores a sense of power, counteracting the helplessness caused by rejection. It's why some people seek revenge or silently wish for the person who rejected them to regret it later. It's not just about wanting to feel better; it's about trying to reclaim control over something that made them feel powerless.

And research backs this up. A 2016 study by Chester and DeWall found that when people imagine retaliating against someone who rejected them, the nucleus accumbens—one of the brain's key reward centers—becomes highly active. In other words, just thinking about revenge gives the brain a dopamine boost, similar to the rush of winning a competition. But here's the catch:

- The feeling is **temporary**. The high from proving yourself or getting revenge doesn't last, which is why people stay stuck in a cycle—constantly chasing the next hit of validation.
- It keeps you **emotionally tied to the rejection**. The more you focus on proving yourself, the more power you give to the very thing that hurt you.
- It **doesn't truly heal the wound**—because the real issue isn't about winning, it's about feeling enough without external validation.

When rejection makes someone feel powerless, their mind instinctively tries to regain control, which can lead to:

- Obsessing over proving your worth to the person who rejected you.
- Needing to "win" against them—whether that's through success, looking better, or proving they made the wrong choice.
- Revenge motivation, where your brain tricks you into thinking payback will give you closure (when in reality, it just keeps you stuck).

Rejection creates an emotional imbalance, and trying to win— whether it's winning an argument, succeeding in life, or even making someone "regret" rejecting you—feels like a way to restore emotional equilibrium. But it's an illusion. The moment

you make your sense of worth dependent on external validation, you stay trapped in a cycle of chasing control—seeking a
high from approval, feeling rejected when it doesn't come, and
spiraling into overthinking all over again.

> *Manipulation is when someone ignores
> their own disrespectful behavior but
> blames you for how you reacted to it.*

REJECTION IN DATING

When someone rejects you, especially someone you deeply desired, there's an unconscious drive to capture the affection of
another elusive person. For many, this rejection often creates
their first experience with true, consciously profound anxiety—a feeling that can embed itself in your emotional framework for years, sometimes life if not addressed. It's true that
rejection can stem from anywhere—a dream job, social circle, or family approval—but in dating, it manifests particularly
powerfully.

You believe securing this new, seemingly unattainable person
will restore your wounded self-worth and reclaim your dig-
nity. Too afraid to walk away, you chase them relentlessly, trying to fill the void left by previous heartbreak and escape that
lingering anxiety that first took root.

The new person becomes a replacement, a stand-in for healing
your original pain. You're not truly seeing them as an individ-

ual, but rather as a remedy for your wounded ego and a shield against that primal anxiety.

The cycle can persist for years, burying itself deep in your subconscious. That initial anxiety becomes the background radiation of your romantic life, as you convince yourself that by "locking down" someone equally difficult to attain, you'll finally overcome the sting of that first rejection and feel whole again.

You can't put a crown on a clown and expect a king.

STOP TAKING IT SO PERSONALLY

You can't do ugly things to people and
expect to live a beautiful life.

When someone mistreats you or leaves you, it's a reflection of them. We don't know their problems, their upbringing, or their experiences. The same applies to perceived rejection. What someone else wants for their life has nothing to do with you. It literally has nothing to do with you. They have their own experiences, their own past, their own hurt, their own desires, and their own needs.

Think about how many times you've seen or experienced someone leaving a good person, only to end up with someone who treats them poorly. Why does this happen? It's not because the abusive person is "better" in any way. It's because the person making this choice is operating from their own unresolved issues and patterns. What people have experienced in life shapes not just what they consciously want, but what they unconsciously believe they need. Sometimes people are drawn to relationships that mirror familiar dynamics, even harmful ones. They might unconsciously seek situations that confirm their existing beliefs about themselves or relationships. The truth is, we might think we know someone, but deep down we don't know all of their experiences or how they have perceived them over time.

The important thing to remember is that someone else's choices don't have anything to do with your worth. When someone chooses a path that seems self-destructive or different to what you believe they should do, they're responding to their own internal world—not making an objective assessment of your value. They're acting from their own reality, not yours. That's why taking someone else's decisions personally is one of the worst mistakes we can make.

Never regret having a good heart.
Everything good comes back to you, multiplied.

Maybe they weren't ready to receive the love and kindness you offered them... maybe they never will be. Maybe they weren't at the emotional level you wanted them to be... maybe they never will be. That's why we have to learn to let go and not take things personally. And then the real question remains... do you actually want someone in your life who doesn't understand true love, care, or friendship? What does that say about how much you value yourself?

When you think logically without the desire to control, or once the feeling of rejection has fully passed, you will see—and probably thank God—that you didn't end up with that person. You just have to believe in who you are again and trust that you can have people in your life who are caring and kind. Most importantly, you'll be just as interested in keeping them in your life as they will be in keeping you in theirs.

You deserve people in your life who make you feel good, but even more so, you have to learn to accept them. The only way to do this is by not allowing your desire for control or wanting to fill that void of your initial perceived rejection to dictate your life. You must reclaim control of yourself and reconnect with who you truly are and what you have to offer.

Understanding the psychology behind our need for control, our fear of rejection, and our desire to "win" is just the first step. Awareness alone isn't enough to create lasting change. Now that we've explored why we react the way we do—how our brains are wired to seek control, avoid rejection, and chase validation—it's time to transform this understanding into practical action. The following strategies aren't quick fixes or temporary bandages. They're evidence-based approaches designed to help you break free from the trap of emotional reactivity, and self-doubt. These solutions target the root causes we've identified, giving you concrete ways to shift from external to internal control, break free from rejection sensitivity, and find fulfillment beyond the need for external validation.

Beautiful souls recognize beautiful souls.
Keep being genuine. Your people will find you.

PART 2

Solutions

REFRAMING CONTROL: FROM EXTERNAL TO INTERNAL

The key to breaking free from the control trap isn't trying harder to manage your external world—it's shifting where you place your attention. Neuroscience reveals that perceived control activates the prefrontal cortex, reducing activity in the amygdala (your brain's alarm system). Even small shifts in what you focus on can dramatically change your experience of stress.

Start by creating a **Control Inventory**. Take a sheet of paper and draw a line down the middle. On the left, list everything currently causing you stress. On the right, identify one aspect of each situation you can directly influence. For example:

- Traffic jam → Your response to the delay
- Someone's opinion of you → How you speak to yourself about it

- Project deadline → How you allocate your time today
- Others' behavior → Your boundaries and reactions

This exercise isn't about positive thinking—it's about neurological efficiency. By redirecting your brain's resources toward actionable areas, you reduce the cognitive load that makes small stressors feel overwhelming.

What's powerful about this approach is that it works even when you're already overwhelmed. When you feel that familiar tension rising—the frustration over a small inconvenience that feels disproportionately upsetting—pause and ask: "What's one thing I can control right now?" Then take one small action from that place of agency. This interrupts the cascade of stress hormones that amplifies your reaction.

BREAKING THE REJECTION-CONTROL CYCLE

*I think some people need to give themselves more credit
for being single instead of feeling like there is always
something wrong. Maybe it just means you're not the type
to settle so easily...there's strength and wisdom in that.*

The fear of rejection is hardwired into your brain. Research by Eisenberger and colleagues revealed that social rejection activates the same neural pathways as physical pain—your brain literally experiences exclusion as a threat to survival. This explains why even minor instances of potential rejection can trigger an overwhelming need to regain control through over-analyzing, seeking validation, or attempting to "win." To break this cycle, you need to address both its neurological and psychological components. From a neurological perspective, the key is regulating your threat response before it hijacks your thinking. When you feel that familiar surge of rejection anxiety, implement the **Emotional Circuit Breaker**:

1. Take a deep breath and acknowledge what's happening: "I'm feeling threatened right now, but I'm actually safe".

2. Ground yourself in the present moment—touch something nearby with intention, look at a specific object in detail, or listen deeply to the sounds around you.

3. Ask yourself, "What do I truly need right now?" before deciding how to respond This works because it gives your prefrontal cortex—the rational part of your brain—time to come back online before you react from your limbic system. Dr. Jill Bolte Taylor's research on the neuroanatomy of emotional reactions demonstrates that emotional reactions require a reset period before rational thinking can resume (Taylor, 2009).

Psychologically, you need to break the pattern of seeking external validation to feel worthy. This requires developing "unconditional self-regard"—a sense of intrinsic value that doesn't depend on others' approval. The most effective way to build this is through the **Values Alignment Practice**. Identify 3-5 core values that matter deeply to you—not what should matter, but what genuinely resonates (perhaps courage, connection, growth, or integrity). When facing rejection or uncertainty, ask yourself: "What would someone who truly lives by these values do right now?" Then take that action with an open heart, regardless of others' responses. This isn't just feel-good advice—it's neurologically sound. When you act from your values, you activate reward pathways in the brain that aren't dependent on external validation. Over time, this creates new neural connections that reduce your vulnerability to rejection sensitivity.

> *Don't expect people to be there for you*
> *just because you're always there for them.*
> *Not everyone has the same heart as you.*

REPLACING THE NEED TO WIN

The drive to "win" after rejection—whether through seeking revenge, proving yourself, or gaining validation—creates a temporary dopamine rush that quickly fades, leaving you still emotionally tied to the very situation that hurt you.

Breaking this addictive cycle requires understanding that the urge to win is actually about regaining a sense of power. You can address this need directly through "approach goals" rather than "avoidance goals"—focusing on moving toward what you want rather than away from what you fear.

When you feel the urge to prove yourself or "win" against someone who hurt you, try the **Redirection Protocol**:

1. Acknowledge the desire for validation or vindication without judgment
2. Ask yourself: "What meaningful goal would give me a genuine sense of agency?"
3. Take one small action toward that goal immediately

Research by Elliot and Thrash (2002) has consistently shown that approach-oriented goals lead to greater psychological well-being, sustained motivation, and reduced rumination compared to avoidance-based motivation strategies that focus on preventing negative outcomes.

This works because it addresses the underlying need for control while breaking the emotional attachment to the source of rejection.

The most powerful shift happens when you redefine winning entirely. True victory isn't about proving yourself to others or gaining external validation—it's about living consciously by your own standards regardless of others' perceptions.

THE INTEGRATION

These approaches aren't just coping mechanisms—they're pathways to fundamentally changing your relationship with control, rejection, and the need for validation. The goal isn't to never feel these impulses but to relate to them differently.

Start small. When you notice yourself reacting to a minor frustration with disproportionate upset, use it as a signal to implement the Control Inventory. When rejection sensitivity arises, practice the Emotional Circuit Breaker before responding. When you feel the urge to "win," apply the Redirection Protocol to channel that energy constructively.

With consistent practice, what begins as conscious effort gradually becomes your natural response. You'll still encounter situations beyond your control, still face rejection, still feel the pull toward external validation—but these experiences will no longer derail you.

The truth is, you were never meant to control everything. You were designed to adapt, to respond creatively, to flow with life rather than constantly fighting to direct it. And in that flexibility, you'll find the genuine security that trying to control everything could never provide.

Some people aren't speaking to you because
they owe you an apology. Read it again.

THE POWER OF REFLECTION: RECOGNIZING YOUR STRENGTH

There's a moment that happens when you truly stop and look back at how far you've come. Not just a casual glance, but a deep, honest reflection. And in that moment, something shifts. You suddenly see yourself not as someone who's struggling, but as someone who has survived.

Look how far you've come. Think back to just a year or two ago. Remember that difficult time when you thought you'd never make it through? When your mind felt so overwhelmed, when escape seemed impossible? Yet here you are. Things might not be perfect—we all have our struggles—but **you got through it, didn't you?**

You see, we forget those moments. And we forget how many of those moments we have had throughout our life. But sometimes when we reflect and remember them, we realize how strong we actually are. And we also realize that often the small things we are worried about don't really matter. Because if you reflect on those moments you never thought you could get out of, it makes you appreciate where you are right now so much more, even if things aren't perfect. At least you're out of that, right?

Sometimes the things that break your heart,
fix your vision.

And if you are currently in one of those moments where you feel like it's one of the worst places in your life, this rule still applies to you. You have been here before. That place that you thought was the hardest time you've ever been through, and you got through. And even though you might say, *"But oh no, this time is very different,"* and maybe it is, but you know what isn't different...**that same spirit that got you through last time.** And I promise you, even though you may not see it right now, that same spirit is going to get you through again. **You are stronger than you give yourself credit for. You are worth more than you believe sometimes.**

Reflection isn't just about looking back at challenges you've overcome. It's also about recognizing the moments of joy, the unexpected blessings, the times when things worked out even when you thought they wouldn't. It's about building a more complete picture of your life—one that includes not just struggles, but also strength, resilience, and moments of unexpected grace.

The more you practice reflection and appreciation, the more you build a reservoir of evidence that you can draw from in difficult times. You start to see patterns. You start to recognize that while life has its ups and downs, you have consistently found ways to navigate them. You start to trust yourself more deeply. And that trust—that bone-deep knowing that you can handle whatever comes—is the foundation of true inner peace.

As you practice recognizing your strength and reflecting on how far you've come, you'll naturally begin to notice something else: the emotional weight you've been carrying that isn't actually yours. Self-reflection doesn't just reveal our inner resilience—it also illuminates the boundaries we've allowed to be crossed, the responsibilities we've unnecessarily assumed, and the emotional burdens we've been carrying for others. Having addressed your relationship with yourself and your experiences, it's time to examine your relationship with others and the invisible weight these connections may be placing on your heart and mind.

The black sheep is sometimes
the only one telling the truth.

PART 3

THE WEIGHT YOU CARRY–BOUNDARIES AND DETACHMENT

CHAPTER 7

The Hidden Cost of Carrying Everyone's Weight

You probably don't even realize **how much you're carrying**. Having your own problems is one thing, but your mind—especially if you're an empathetic and caring person—can be cluttered with things that aren't even yours to hold. Other people's problems, their moods, their expectations, and their energy are all very real. You absorb it all, feeling it so deeply that it starts to weigh on you, even when no one has directly asked you to take it on.

At first, being there for others feels like a choice—a natural extension of who you are. You don't mind being the person people turn to, the one who listens, the one who supports. But over time, something shifts. What began as a choice transforms into an obligation. You start to notice that you're always the strong one, but when you need strength, no one is there. You start to feel drained, overwhelmed, and even a little lost.

*People who can't communicate think
everything is an argument.*

It's not just about helping with concrete problems. It's the way their energy lingers in your own emotions. The way someone's stress becomes your stress, how their sadness seeps into your day. It's the way you replay conversations, wondering if you could have done more, said more, been more. The feeling of wanting to get off the phone to someone, but feeling guilty for cutting them off. It's the pressure of feeling like you're never giving enough, never quite meeting an invisible standard that no one else is even holding themselves to. But at what point do you stop and ask: **Who is carrying me?**

SELF-ASSESSMENT: THE WEIGHT YOU CARRY

*Only people who aren't happy with themselves
are mean to others. Always remember that.*

Before we go deeper, take a moment to reflect on your relationships. For each important person in your life, ask yourself:

- Do I feel energized or drained after spending time with them?
- When I'm struggling, do they show up for me the way I show up for them?
- If I stopped initiating contact, would this relationship continue?

- Do I often feel resentful about how much I give versus how little I receive?

The answers to these questions will tell you everything you need to know.

> *Sometimes it's your friends that keep*
> *your enemies updated. Be careful.*

THE WEIGHT OF OTHERS

This all leads onto another point...You weren't meant to be the emotional dumping ground for everyone around you. You weren't meant to put your own needs on the back burner just so other people can be comfortable. And yet, that's exactly what's happening every time you push down your own emotions to make space for someone else's, every time you sacrifice your energy, your time, your mental well-being to solve problems that aren't yours, and **every time you set yourself on fire to keep someone else warm**.

Think about how much of your energy goes into things that don't actually belong to you: You feel responsible for making sure everyone around you is happy. You feel guilty for saying no, even when you're exhausted. You absorb other people's problems, even when they never asked for your help. You take on the role of the peacemaker, even in situations that aren't yours to fix. *This isn't kindness—this is self-abandonment.* When you constantly sacrifice your well-being for others' comfort, you're not being generous—you're participating in your own depletion.

They don't involve you, don't get involved.
They don't tell you, don't ask. They don't invite you,
don't go. Know your position in people's lives.

Trauma researcher Charles Figley recognized this pattern so clearly that he gave it a name: "compassion fatigue"—a condition that mirrors clinical burnout in people who constantly take on others' emotional burdens (Figley, 2002). His research showed that those who regularly absorb others' pain eventually develop symptoms almost identical to post-traumatic stress, including emotional exhaustion, detachment, and a diminished sense of accomplishment or meaning. This scientific finding validates what you've felt all along—**carrying everyone else's emotional weight isn't just taxing; it's actively harmful to your wellbeing**.

And here's the hardest part to accept: People will keep letting you do it. They will keep coming to you, keep relying on you, keep unloading on you—because they know you'll take it. Not necessarily because they're bad people, but because you've made it so easy for them. They don't have to carry their own weight because you always step in before they ever feel the need to. But while they're getting lighter, you're getting heavier. Their problems sit on your shoulders. Their emotions drain your energy. And slowly, without realizing it, you lose yourself in other people's lives, while yours starts to feel like an afterthought.

It doesn't matter whether these people are meant for you or not. If you're always making their well-being your own responsibility, then at some point, you have to ask yourself: *What is this doing to me?* Because love shouldn't feel like exhaustion. Supporting someone shouldn't feel like losing yourself in the process.

> *Stay away from people who act like a victim
> in the problem they've created.*

ONE-SIDED RELATIONSHIPS AND THE CYCLE OF FALSE HOPE

It's a recurring pattern, isn't it? You convince yourself that if you just give a little more—more time, more effort, more understanding—things will change. That if you're patient enough, supportive enough, forgiving enough, people will finally appreciate you the way you deserve. But no matter how much you give, it's never enough. **You're always the one putting in the effort. You're always the one who cares more.** And in return? You don't get it back the way you give it.

At first, you don't even notice the imbalance. You tell yourself that relationships require effort, that being there for people is a good thing. And it is—until you realize that the effort isn't being returned. That you're the one always checking in, always reaching out, always making sure the connection stays alive. That if you stopped trying, the relationship would probably disappear altogether. And that realization stings. Because it forces you to see something you don't want to admit: *some people only keep you around because you make their life easier, not because they truly value you.*

> Respectfully, I don't go above and beyond for
> people anymore. I meet you as far as you meet me.
> I speak to you as much as you speak to me.
> I include you as much as you include me.
> I'm done being extra for people.

The problem is, when you're someone who naturally gives, you don't think about keeping score. You don't expect anything in return—at least, not at first. You assume that your kindness, your generosity, your presence will eventually be appreciated. That people will notice how much you do for them and reciprocate out of their own goodwill. But that's not how it works. Not everyone values effort. Not everyone sees your kindness as something worth matching.

So you hold onto hope—the belief that if you just wait a little longer, invest a little more, tolerate just a bit more pain, things will turn around. You replay every excuse they've given, every promise they've made, every glimpse of potential they've shown—convincing yourself that change is just around the corner. But it never comes. Maybe they apologize, but nothing actually improves. Maybe they say they'll try, but you end up in the same exhausting cycle, waiting for something that never happens.

Back in the 1980s, researchers Prochaska and DiClemente studied thousands of people trying to make difficult personal changes. What they discovered was revolutionary: meaningful personal transformation follows predictable stages, but crucially, **it only happens when someone has developed their own internal motivation—never because someone else wants them to change** (Prochaska & DiClemente, 1983). Their Stages of Change model explains why your hope that someone will change because you want them to badly enough is fundamentally misplaced.

Some people will take and take and take, without a second thought. Not because they're evil, but because you've made it easy for them. You've set the standard that they don't have to do anything, and they've happily accepted that role. They don't ask how you're doing. They don't offer support when you need it. They don't put in effort—because they don't have to. They know you'll always be the one who does.

The reason it's so hard to let go isn't just because you love them—it's because you're emotionally invested in the idea of them. *The version of them that exists in your mind.* The person they could be if they just put in the effort. But the person you're holding onto—the one you're waiting for—only exists in your imagination. **The real version of them, the one who refuses to change, is the one who keeps hurting you.**

THE COST TO YOUR HEALTH

Carrying everyone else's weight doesn't just exhaust you emotionally—it physically wears you down. Research has shown that empathic overload actually triggers the same stress responses in your body as if you were experiencing the stressors directly. Your body doesn't distinguish between your pain and the pain you absorb from others—it responds with the same cascade of stress hormones either way.

You feel tired all the time, even when you get enough sleep. Your body aches. Your mind feels foggy. Your immune system weakens. Stress builds up in ways you don't even recognize until one day, **you just don't have anything left to give**. And the sad reality is, when you finally hit that point, the people you've carried won't know how to help you—because they never had to before.

Studies show that chronic emotional caretaking is linked to increased risk of anxiety, depression, sleep disturbances, anger, and even physical health issues like headaches, gastrointestinal problems, and high blood pressure. *Your body keeps the score of the emotional labor you're doing, even when your mind tries to push through.* The physical manifestations of carrying others' burdens aren't in your imagination—they're documented physiological responses to prolonged emotional stress.

> *Your anger has always been a reflection of how*
> *hurt you are. Nobody understands that.*

Eventually, you reach a breaking point. You feel drained, but you tell yourself it's just part of life. You feel overwhelmed, but you convince yourself that it's your job to handle everything. You feel resentful, but instead of stepping back, you keep giving, keep fixing, keep absorbing. Until one day, you wake up and realize—**this isn't sustainable. This isn't how life is supposed to feel.**

The journey to reclaim your energy and establish healthier boundaries begins with this recognition. It's not selfish to prioritize your wellbeing—it's necessary. Because the truth is, you cannot effectively care for others when you're depleted. *Real compassion must include compassion for yourself.* And sometimes, the most loving thing you can do—both for yourself and ultimately for others—is to stop carrying what was never yours to carry in the first place.

Inevitably, the weight of carrying everyone else's emotions and problems leads to this critical question: How do you put down this burden without drowning in guilt? Because the moment you try to reclaim your energy and establish healthier patterns, you encounter perhaps the most powerful force keeping you trapped—the voice that whispers you're selfish for prioritizing yourself. Let's explore how guilt becomes the invisible chain that prevents you from setting the boundaries you desperately need.

CHAPTER 8

The Power of Guilt and the Struggle to Set Boundaries

Nothing annoys me more than when someone expects you to be okay with something that they wouldn't be okay with if it was done to them.

Setting boundaries shouldn't be hard. It shouldn't come with a wave of guilt, second-guessing, or the fear that you're letting people down. But for some reason, it does. Every time you say no, every time you express what you need, every time you refuse to tolerate something that drains you, that familiar guilt creeps in, whispering:

"Are you being selfish?" "What if they get upset?" "What if they think you don't care?"

And before you know it, you're back to saying yes when you don't mean it. You're back to over-explaining, over-apologizing, and overextending yourself just to avoid the discomfort that comes with setting limits.

Guilt has a way of making you question everything. It makes you feel responsible for how others will feel if you don't meet their expectations. It tells you that if you cared, you would stay, keep trying, keep giving—even if it's breaking you. One reason guilt is so powerful is because of something called the Sunk Cost Fallacy—a psychological tendency to keep investing in something simply because you've already put so much time, energy, or emotion into it. The more you've given, the harder it is to walk away. Your brain tells you, *But I've already spent years in this relationship. I've already tried so hard to make this friendship work. I've already given so much of myself—if I leave now, wasn't it all a waste?*

This guilt extends to the process of growth itself. No one tells you how much guilt comes with growth—the better you become, the harder it gets to stay in places that no longer align with you. It's a strange kind of grief—to love someone, to have shared years of laughter, support, and connection, yet to feel yourself slowly drifting away. This guilt comes from the idea that you owe people the version of you they once knew. That because they were there for you in the past, you should keep showing up in the same way, even when it no longer feels right.

> *Stop overplaying your role!*
> *Deal with people how they deal with you:*
> *hardly, barely, and accordingly.*

HOW INVISIBLE BOUNDARIES ENABLE DISAPPOINTMENT

This cycle of hope and disappointment is further enabled by your lack of boundaries. People don't automatically know how to treat you—you show them. Every time you tolerate something that makes you uncomfortable, every time you bite your tongue instead of speaking up, every time you say yes when you really mean no, you send a message. And the message is this: *My feelings don't matter. My needs don't matter. You can treat me however you want, and I will accept it.*

It doesn't start all at once. It starts small—letting someone interrupt you, letting a friend cancel on you repeatedly without explanation, letting a partner talk to you in a way that makes you feel uneasy. You brush it off, tell yourself it's not a big deal. But over time, it builds. The more you allow, the more they take. And before you know it, you're in relationships where your boundaries don't exist, where you feel drained, used, or even invisible—because you never made it clear that your needs mattered in the first place.

This is the hard truth: People will only respect the boundaries that you enforce. If you don't set limits, people won't magically stop taking advantage of your time, energy, and kindness. Not necessarily because they're bad people, but because you've never given them a reason to think otherwise.

Some people are really so delusional that they
think it's disrespectful when you don't just sit back
and allow them to continue to disrespect you.

When you don't set boundaries, you become the person who is always available, always agreeable, always sacrificing. And while that might make you seem "easygoing" or "low-maintenance" on the surface, deep down, it's killing you. It's exhausting to constantly put yourself last. It's frustrating to always be the one adjusting, compromising, and making things easier for others while no one does the same for you.

Why is it so hard to set boundaries? For many, it comes down to fear—fear of upsetting people, fear of being seen as difficult, fear of being abandoned. You worry that if you start saying no, people will leave. You worry that if you stand up for yourself, you'll be judged. The pioneering work of John Bowlby on attachment theory helps explain why these fears run so deep. His decades of research revealed how our earliest childhood experiences form templates for all our future relationships. If your early experiences taught you that expressing needs or setting limits would somehow get you rejected or punished, you likely developed an insecure attachment style that makes boundary-setting feel terrifying even decades later (Bowlby, 1988). And maybe you've been conditioned to believe that keeping the peace is more important than protecting your own well-being.

But here's what you need to understand: The people who truly respect and care about you won't be angry when you set boundaries. They will adjust. The ones who get upset? They're the ones who benefited from you having none.

> *They are not grown until they know*
> *how to communicate, apologize and accept*
> *accountability without blaming someone else.*

Once you understand how guilt keeps you trapped in boundary-less relationships, you face an even more subtle challenge. It's not just about setting boundaries—it's about what happens after. Why do we feel compelled to justify every limit we set? Why do we over-explain our growth to people who haven't earned that level of access to our inner world? The next stage of reclaiming your power requires learning when to stop explaining and simply let go.

CHAPTER 9

The Trap of Over-Explaining and Letting Go

Sometimes you just have to be done.
Not mad, not upset... Just done.

As you begin to recognize the weight you've been carrying and start setting boundaries, you face a new challenge: the compulsion to over-explain your decisions and justify your growth. You've been conditioned to believe that every decision you make should come with an acceptable reason, one that's digestible enough for others to approve of. *You've been taught that if someone is upset with you, you must explain yourself until they understand.* That if you change, if you outgrow something, if you simply don't want to do something anymore, you must have a "good enough" excuse.

Think about how much time you've wasted over-explaining your actions to people who weren't even entitled to an answer. How many times you've justified walking away from something that no longer felt right for you. How many times you've softened the truth just to avoid making someone uncomfortable. Did they ever really accept your explanation? Or did they just argue with it, try to make you feel guilty, or twist it into something else?

The power of silence isn't about cutting people off—it's about reclaiming your peace. It's about refusing to be dragged into unnecessary drama, refusing to argue over things that don't matter, refusing to let someone else's issues become your burden. Silence is uncomfortable. It forces people to sit with their own actions without the distraction of your emotions. It strips them of the power they once had over you—the ability to provoke, manipulate, and twist your words.

> *Another problem with having a big heart is that sometimes people think you're stupid. Until you cut them off...and they'll still find a way to blame you.*

Some people only understand your value when they no longer have access to you. The moment you stop engaging, the moment you stop giving them a reaction, you force them to feel the absence of you. *Silence speaks in a way that words never can.* Words can be argued with, twisted, ignored. But silence? Silence lingers. Silence leaves room for reflection. Silence forces them to confront the fact that you're done.

LETTING GO... OF YOURSELF

There's a version of you that got you here. A version of you that survived, that adapted, that learned how to navigate life in the only way it knew how. That version of you cared too much, overthought everything, took on burdens that weren't theirs to carry. That version of you kept people around even when they drained you. That version of you bent over backward to be liked, to be chosen, to feel worthy. That version of you sacrificed their own peace just to keep other people comfortable.

Letting go of people is hard, but letting go of yourself— the self you've known for so long—that's something else entirely. You've spent years identifying with your patterns, your fears, your emotional reactions. You've spent so much time being the person who overthinks, who takes things personally, who spirals over the smallest things, that the idea of not doing that almost feels foreign. Who are you without the worry? Without the need for control? Without the constant pull of guilt?

Letting go of the old version of you is terrifying because, for a long time, that version protected you. Maybe overthinking kept you safe from disappointment. Maybe people-pleasing helped you avoid conflict. Maybe staying in toxic cycles gave you a false sense of security. Even the things that hurt you served a purpose at one point.

The problem is, *growth feels like loss before it feels like freedom.* You start recognizing your old patterns, and part of you doesn't want to let them go. You start setting boundaries, and it feels unnatural. You stop over-explaining yourself, and you feel rude. You stop engaging in drama, and you feel disconnected. You stop chasing people, and you feel alone.

But this discomfort is temporary. The more you practice letting go—of explanations, of guilt, of the need to be understood by everyone—the lighter you'll feel. You'll start to realize that true freedom comes not from having everyone approve of your choices, but from being at peace with them yourself. True freedom doesn't just mean letting go of people who no longer have a place in your future, it's letting go of the version of yourself that accepted it.

> *Stop sitting at the table where they speak evil about others, because when you get up, you are the topic.*

PART 3

Solutions

RECLAIMING YOUR EMOTIONAL AUTONOMY

The first step toward freedom is understanding that carrying everyone else's emotional weight isn't compassion—it's a learned pattern that likely began long before you had the words to describe it. Research in developmental psychology shows that many over-givers were once children who learned that their worth was tied to how well they could attend to others' needs (Miller, 1981). This isn't your fault, but recognizing the pattern is now your responsibility.

> *Blocking, unfollowing or unfriending someone doesn't mean you're weak and can't handle your emotions. It can just mean you're sick of their garbage and want them as far away from your life as possible.*

Start with the **Energy Exchange Audit**. For one week, track every significant interaction and note three things:

1. How you felt before the interaction (energized, neutral, depleted)
2. What emotional weight you absorbed during the interaction
3. How you felt afterward

Look for patterns. Which relationships consistently leave you drained? Which interactions involve you carrying emotional burdens that aren't yours? This isn't about judging others—it's about seeing clearly where your energy is going.

Once you've identified these patterns, implement what psychologists call "compassionate detachment"—the ability to care deeply without absorbing others' emotional states. When someone brings their problems to you, practice the **Compassionate Container** technique:

Imagine their emotions as water. Rather than absorbing this water into your own being (as you've habitually done), visualize creating a beautiful, respectful container to hold it temporarily. You can see it clearly, honor its presence, offer genuine care—but it remains in its container, separate from your own emotional state.

As you practice this visualization, you can add these verbal boundaries if you feel the need:

- "I'm here to listen, but I may not have solutions."
- "I can hold space for you without taking this on as my responsibility."

- "I care about you while still maintaining my own emotional balance."

What makes this approach powerful is that it doesn't require you to stop caring. It simply changes how you care, allowing you to be present without becoming emotionally fused with others' experiences. Neuroscience research confirms that this type of mindful compassion activates different neural networks than emotional contagion—the former associated with resilience and positive emotions, the latter with burnout and emotional exhaustion (Singer & Klimecki, 2014).

Stop oversharing - privacy is power.

SETTING BOUNDARIES WITHOUT GUILT

Setting proper boundaries starts by understanding the "guilt-to-boundary" cycle. When you feel guilty about enforcing a limit, your brain is essentially experiencing withdrawal from its habitual pattern. This discomfort feels unbearable in the moment, prompting you to abandon your boundary to relieve the guilt.

Breaking this cycle requires implementing the **Boundary Reinforcement System**:

First, prepare your boundaries in advance. Rather than creating them in the heat of the moment (when emotions are high and resolve is low), decide beforehand what limits you need in different contexts:

- Time boundaries: When you're available and when you're not
- Emotional boundaries: What kinds of support you can offer
- Physical boundaries: What feels comfortable in terms of energy and space
- Mental boundaries: What topics or dynamics you won't engage with

Disrespect can permanently shut doors that apologies cannot reopen. Consider this carefully.

Next, focus on clearly communicating your boundaries. Many people struggle not just with having boundaries, but with expressing them effectively. Remember that boundaries aren't ultimatums or threats—they're simply statements of what you need to feel safe, respected, and emotionally balanced.

Start by communicating your boundaries calmly and directly when they first arise. You don't need to wait until you're overwhelmed or resentful. When someone makes a request or behaves in a way that crosses your limits, address it immediately but kindly. Be specific about what isn't working for you and what you need instead.

If people respect your initial communication, wonderful. However, many find that despite clear communication, some people continue to overstep. When this happens, it's important to recognize that this is no longer about your communication skills—it's about the other person's unwillingness to respect your needs. At this point, you may need to be more direct and use concise, unambiguous language.

Effective boundaries are clear, calm, and consistent. They don't require lengthy explanations or apologies. Practice statements like:

- "I can listen for the next 20 minutes, and then I need to focus on my work."
- "I'm not comfortable discussing that topic."
- "I need some time to myself this evening."
- "This doesn't work for me."

When guilt inevitably arises after setting a boundary, implement the **Guided Guilt Release**:

1. Acknowledge the guilt without judgment: "I notice I'm feeling guilty right now."
2. Remind yourself: "This feeling is temporary. It's my brain adjusting to a new pattern."
3. Focus on your breathing until the intensity passes.
4. Affirm your right to self-care: "Having boundaries doesn't make me selfish—it makes me balanced and sustainable."

Research on habit formation shows that neural pathways weaken when not reinforced and strengthen with consistent use. Each time you maintain a boundary despite feeling guilty, you're literally rewiring your brain to associate boundary-setting with self-respect rather than guilt.

This approach is particularly effective for those struggling with "people-pleasing dependency"—a condition where self-worth becomes contingent on others' approval. By gradually separating your actions from others' reactions, you reclaim your autonomy while still maintaining genuine care for those around you.

BREAKING FREE FROM ONE-SIDED RELATIONSHIPS

You can't hurt someone constantly and expect their energy to be the same. Even people with good hearts have limits.

One of the most painful realizations on this journey is that some relationships exist primarily because of what you give, not because of mutual value or respect. This doesn't mean these people are necessarily malicious—often they're simply responding to the dynamic you've established. But once you see this pattern clearly, continuing these relationships in their current form becomes impossible.

The **Reciprocity Reset** is a structured approach to transforming or releasing these one-sided dynamics:

First, implement a temporary **Giving Fast**. For 7-14 days, stop initiating contact, stop offering help before being asked, and stop going above and beyond in these identified relationships. This isn't about playing games or testing people—it's about creating space to see the relationship's true nature when your over-functioning is removed.

During this period, journal about what you observe. Does the relationship continue without your extra effort? Do they check on you with the same care you've shown them? Does the dynamic feel different when you're not overextending?

Based on what you discover, make a conscious decision about each relationship:

Option 1: Renegotiate - For relationships worth preserving, have a direct conversation about creating more balance. This isn't about demands or accusations, but honest expression:

- "I've realized I tend to give more than is sustainable for me."
- "I'd like to create a relationship where we both feel supported."
- "Here's what support looks like to me..."

Option 2: Accept With Clear Limits - Some relationships may continue with adjusted expectations. You might decide certain family relationships or longstanding friendships are worth maintaining with firm boundaries around what you will and won't provide emotionally.

Option 3: Release - Some relationships simply cannot survive the withdrawal of your over-functioning. While painful, releasing these connections is sometimes the only path to your wellbeing.

What makes this approach different from typical "cut them off" advice is that it's based on observation rather than reaction. You're making conscious choices based on what you actually see, not what you fear or hope might happen.

Avoid people who are close to people who dislike you.
They are dangerous.

EMBRACING THE EMPTY SPACE

Perhaps the most challenging phase of this journey is navigating the emptiness that comes when you stop filling your life with other people's needs, drama, and emotions. This void is temporary but crucial—it's the space where your authentic self begins to emerge.

Psychologist Carl Jung called this the "creative void"—the necessary emptiness that precedes genuine transformation. Rather than rushing to fill this space with new relationships or distractions, learning to sit with it comfortably is essential for lasting change.

The **Void Navigation Protocol** provides structure for this ambiguous time:

First, normalize the discomfort. The emptiness feels threatening because your nervous system interprets the unfamiliar as dangerous. Research in neuroscience shows that novel situations activate the brain's threat-detection system, triggering anxiety even when no actual danger exists. Remind yourself: "This emptiness isn't harmful—it's unfamiliar. My brain is registering the unfamiliar as threatening, but I am safe."

Next, implement daily **Self-Connection Practices**. When your identity has been built around others' needs, connecting with your own becomes a skill to develop:

- Mindful body scans to reconnect with physical sensations
- Journaling to identify your authentic preferences without others' influence
- Small experiments with choices based solely on your desires rather than others' expectations

Finally, resist the urge to rush this phase. Research on transition psychology indicates that premature closure—filling the void before genuine transformation occurs—often leads to repeating old patterns in new contexts. Give yourself permission to exist in this in-between state, knowing that what's emerging is worth the temporary discomfort.

THE LIBERATION OF LETTING GO

The final step in this process is perhaps the most counterintuitive: releasing the need for others to understand your journey. The compulsion to over-explain your boundaries, your growth, or your decisions comes from the same pattern of prioritizing others' comfort over your own truth.

Implement the **Minimal Explanation Policy**:

- For casual relationships: "This doesn't work for me" is a complete sentence.
- For closer relationships: "I'm making changes to support my wellbeing" provides context without inviting debate.
- For essential relationships: "I care about our connection and I need to make these changes. I'm happy to answer specific questions, but I won't defend my need for these boundaries."

What makes this approach powerful is that it honors both your need for authentic expression and your right to privacy around your healing process. Not everyone has earned access to your inner world, and not everyone will understand your journey—nor do they need to.

THE INTEGRATION

These practices aren't separate techniques but interconnected elements of a new way of being. Start with the Energy Exchange Audit to see clearly where your energy is going. Practice the Compassionate Container technique when others bring their problems to you. Implement the Boundary Reinforcement System when guilt arises. Use the Reciprocity Reset to transform or release one-sided relationships. Navigate the creative void with patience and self-connection. And embrace the freedom of minimal explanations.

With consistent practice, what once felt like betrayal—prioritizing your own wellbeing—gradually becomes your natural state. You'll discover that true generosity can only flow from abundance, not depletion. That authentic connections thrive with healthy boundaries, not endless accommodation. That your worth was never tied to how much you could carry for others, but to your inherent value as a human being.

The journey isn't about becoming selfish or cold. It's about creating a life where giving comes from choice rather than compulsion. Where love doesn't cost you your wellbeing. Where you finally understand that carrying your own heart with tenderness is the most important responsibility you have—and the foundation for any genuine care you offer to others.

Now that you understand the struggle of letting go and the challenge of over-explaining, it's time to recognize a deeper truth: sometimes the relationships you're trying to navigate aren't just difficult—they're deliberately manipulative. The next chapter reveals how to identify when someone is systematically undermining your reality, and why this recognition is the first critical step toward genuine freedom.

PART 4

THE BREAKING POINT– RECOGNITION AND REALIZATION

CHAPTER 10

Hidden Manipulation: Recognizing When Others Make You the Problem

Never try to defend yourself against a narcissist.
They already know you're right, they just
want you to go crazy trying to prove it.

It starts subtly. A comment here, a dismissive reaction there. You bring up something that hurt you, and instead of getting an apology, you get a confused look and a response like, *That never happened.* Or maybe it did happen, but you're told you're overreacting, too sensitive, or reading into things too much. At first, you might question yourself—*Did I misinterpret that? Am I making a big deal out of nothing?* But over time, the doubt grows, and before you know it, you're questioning your own reality.

This is gaslighting—the psychological manipulation that makes you second-guess your thoughts, emotions,

and even your memory of events. It's not just someone disagreeing with you or having a different perspective. It's someone actively making you feel like your experiences aren't valid, like your feelings are an inconvenience, and like *you* are the problem for even bringing them up. Gaslighting can happen in any type of relationship—romantic, friendships, family, even at work. It's one of the most toxic forms of manipulation because it's designed to make you doubt yourself to the point where you no longer trust your own judgment. And when you stop trusting yourself, it becomes easier for someone else to control the narrative.

> *Narcissists be like: How dare you ruin my reputation by telling people things I did and said.*

The most dangerous part? Gaslighting doesn't just make you question the situation—it makes you question yourself. You start wondering if maybe you do overreact. If maybe you do expect too much. If maybe you really are the problem. And once that doubt takes hold, it becomes harder to stand up for yourself because you're no longer sure if your feelings are even valid.

One of the biggest red flags of gaslighting is when someone refuses to acknowledge your feelings. Instead of listening, they dismiss, minimize, or flip the conversation back on you. They might say things like:

You're imagining things.
You're just being dramatic.

You always have to start a fight over nothing.
I never said that.
Why do you always take things the wrong way?
You're remembering it wrong.

Notice how none of these responses actually address what you're feeling? Instead of taking accountability, they shift the focus to making you feel like you're wrong for even bringing it up. And that's the entire goal of gaslighting: To make you feel so unsure of yourself that you stop questioning them altogether.

When people know they did you wrong they avoid you.

WHEN PERPETRATORS PRETEND TO BE VICTIMS

You're crazy to everyone who can't manipulate you.

But gaslighting isn't the only tactic people use to manipulate you. Some people will hurt you and then act like you hurt them. They will betray your trust, lie, manipulate, or treat you unfairly, and when you finally call them out or walk away, suddenly they're the one suffering. Suddenly, they're the victim, and you're the cruel one for not tolerating their behavior anymore.

This is one of the most frustrating and emotionally draining experiences to go through—when the person who caused the

117

damage twists the story to make themselves look innocent while making you look like the problem. It's not just manipulation; it's a complete rewriting of reality.

So why do people do this? Why do some people refuse to take responsibility and instead play the victim in situations where they are clearly at fault?

1. To Avoid Accountability

Taking responsibility for their actions would require them to face the truth—that they were wrong, that they hurt someone, and that they should change. But change is uncomfortable, and accountability requires effort. It's easier to flip the script. Instead of acknowledging what they did, they make you seem like the unreasonable one for reacting to their behavior.

Maybe you got upset because they lied to you. Instead of apologizing, they say, *I can't believe you're making such a big deal out of this. You're always trying to find a reason to be mad at me.* Maybe they ignored your boundaries, and when you finally put your foot down, they say, *You're being so cold and distant. I don't know why you're treating me this way.* Maybe they consistently took advantage of your kindness, and when you finally stop catering to them, they say, *I guess you never really cared about me at all.*

Notice what's happening? They're not addressing what they did. They're not apologizing. They're making your reaction the problem instead of their behavior. This is a classic manipulation tactic to avoid taking responsibility.

2. To Control the Narrative

The moment they sense that they might lose power over you, they rewrite the story. And in their version, they are the victim, and you are the villain.

They'll exaggerate details, conveniently leave out key moments, or completely twist the truth to make themselves look like the innocent one. Suddenly, they were just trying to help, and you overreacted. Suddenly, they didn't mean to hurt you, and you're unfairly attacking them.

And if they can get other people to believe their story? Even better. They will tell anyone who will listen how much you've hurt them, how they just don't understand why you've changed, how they did everything for you, and this is how you repay them. They want sympathy. They want attention. Most of all, they want to make sure that no one sees the truth about what actually happened.

> *Be careful what you hear about somebody. You might be hearing it from the problem.*

3. Because They Genuinely Believe Their Own Lies

Some people aren't just pretending to be the victim—they truly see themselves that way. They are so disconnected from their own actions that they don't even recognize the harm they've caused. In their mind, they can do no wrong. Any time something goes wrong in their life, it's always someone else's fault. They refuse to reflect, refuse to self-analyze, and refuse to grow.

These types of people live in a state of perpetual victimhood, where the world is always against them. No matter what happens, they see themselves as the one who was wronged—even when they were the one causing the harm. If you confront them, they won't see it as an opportunity for self-awareness. They'll see it as an attack. And instead of listening, they will immediately go on the defensive, painting you as the aggressor for daring to hold them accountable.

4. To Manipulate Your Emotions

The most dangerous thing about people who play the victim is that they know how to make you doubt yourself. They use your empathy against you, making you feel guilty for standing up for yourself.

They'll cry. They'll talk about how hard their life has been. They'll bring up every struggle they've ever gone through, making you feel like you're being too harsh or too unforgiving. And because you don't want to be the bad guy, you soften. You second-guess yourself. You start to wonder if maybe you really are being unfair.

This is exactly what they want. Because the moment you doubt yourself, you give them back their power. You let them escape accountability. You fall back into the pattern of accepting their behavior because you don't want to hurt them. But the truth is, they don't care about how they've hurt you—they only care about controlling how you respond to it.

Not one scar on my heart came from an enemy.
They all came from people who claimed to
love me the most.

5. Because It's Always Worked Before

People who play the victim do so because it has always worked for them. It's a pattern they've repeated over and over, and if it has kept them from taking responsibility in the past, why would they stop now?

They've learned that if they cry, if they act wounded, if they make enough of a scene, people will side with them. They've learned that as long as they look like the victim, no one will question what they actually did to cause the situation in the first place. And if they can manipulate you into feeling guilty, if they can make you question yourself, then they win. They get to walk away without consequences, while you sit there wondering if maybe you really are the bad guy.

These behaviors are called 'psychological projections' - defense mechanisms identified by Sigmund Freud and further developed by researchers like George E. Vaillant (1992). When someone projects their own negative behaviors onto you, they're unconsciously transferring unacceptable feelings or actions to protect their self-image. Research in cognitive psychology has shown that this self-deception allows people to maintain a positive self-concept despite engaging in harmful behaviors (Bandura, 1999). By casting themselves as victims, they resolve the cognitive dissonance between their actions and their desired self-image as good people.

> *You can't keep getting mad at people for sucking*
> *the life out of you if you keep giving them*
> *the straw. Protect your peace... leave.*

RECOGNIZING MANIPULATION AND RECLAIMING YOUR REALITY

So how do you recognize when you're being manipulated in these ways? One sign is when you feel worse after every conversation. You start out upset about something, but by the end, instead of feeling heard, you feel confused, guilty, or like you need to apologize—even though you were the one who had a valid concern.

Another sign is that you've stopped trusting your own emotions. You hesitate before speaking up because you worry you'll just be told you're overreacting again. You replay conversations in your head, wondering if you're the one in the wrong. You second-guess your own experiences because the other person seems so sure that you're mistaken.

The most important thing to remember is this: Your feelings are real. Your experiences are real. If something upset you, it matters. Someone who genuinely cares about you won't try to convince you otherwise—they will listen, even if they don't agree.

> *Some people have to pretend you're a bad person so they don't feel guilty about the things they did to you.*

So to recap, this is how you recognize when it's time to distance yourself from manipulative dynamics:

First, notice the pattern of doubt. If after interactions you consistently feel confused about your own perceptions, this isn't coincidental—it's a deliberate erosion of your reality.

Second, document the reality-distortion. When someone consistently rewrites history, start keeping records. Create a private journal of actual events. Not to prove anything to them (which rarely works), but to maintain your own grip on reality amid their contradictions.

Third, watch for the moment when defending your perspective becomes your full-time job. When you find yourself exhausted from constantly having to validate your own experiences, that's not a communication problem—it's a manipulation problem.

And finally, recognize that clarity often comes only with distance. Sometimes you can't see the full extent of manipulation until you're no longer immersed in it. This isn't about boundaries alone—it's about preserving your fundamental right to trust your own perception of reality.

When dealing with someone who plays the victim, trust your own reality. If someone is making you feel like you're crazy, pause and ask yourself: What actually happened? Stick to the facts. Don't let them rewrite the story.

Refuse to engage in their guilt trips. If they start playing the victim to avoid accountability, don't fall for it. If they were truly sorry, they would own up to their actions, not twist the narrative. Recognize that some people will never change. You will never get through to someone who refuses to see their own patterns. Stop wasting your energy trying to make them understand. Because once you stop questioning yourself, once you stop letting someone else rewrite your reality, you take your power back. And that is something no manipulator wants to see.

> *Nobody gets angrier than a narcissist being*
> *accused of something they definitely did.*

Once you can recognize manipulation for what it is, you'll eventually reach a pivotal moment—the breaking point where awareness transforms into action. This isn't just about identifying unhealthy patterns anymore; it's about finding the clarity and courage to finally say "enough."

CHAPTER 11

The Last Time They'll Make You Feel This Way: Knowing When to Walk Away

Sorry but someone who destroys your mental health CANNOT be the love of your life.

There comes a moment when you just know. Maybe it's not dramatic. Maybe it's not some big explosion. Maybe there isn't even a final conversation. It's just a feeling. A quiet realization that you can't do this anymore. That you've been waiting, hoping, excusing, explaining—over and over again. And for what? Another disappointment? Another excuse? Another cycle that leads you right back to the same feeling—hurt, drained, unseen?

You tell yourself that maybe this time will be different. Maybe they'll finally understand. Maybe they'll wake up and realize what they have. Maybe if you just explain it one more time, they'll get it. But they never do. They never really hear you.

They just do the bare minimum to keep you holding on, just enough to keep you hoping. And every time, you convince yourself to stay a little longer, to give them another chance, to shrink yourself just a little more so they don't feel uncomfortable with your needs.

But one day, something shifts. Maybe it's a small moment, something that wouldn't have seemed like a big deal before. A comment that feels different this time. A silence that speaks louder than words. A realization that you're not even shocked anymore—*you're just tired.* Tired of feeling like you're the only one who cares enough to fix things. Tired of being in a relationship, a friendship, a situation that only seems to take from you, never give. Tired of holding onto the idea of who they could be instead of accepting who they really are.

And that's when it hits you: **this is the last time.**

The last time they make you feel unworthy. The last time you let their inconsistency mess with your peace. The last time you let their own insecurities make you doubt yourself. The last time you give them access to your heart when they haven't proven they deserve it. The last time you believe in the potential of someone instead of looking at their actual actions.

Because this time, you're not just saying you're done. You actually are.

Walking away doesn't always mean there's some big betrayal. *Sometimes, the deepest pain comes from realizing that someone you cared about just doesn't have the capacity to meet you where you are.*

That they don't love you in the way you need to be loved. That they are not willing to change, no matter how many times they say they will. And that's hard to accept—because it means letting go of the version of them you had in your head.

Often times we get called crazy for assuming
things that turned out to be true.

You have to grieve the hope you held onto. You have to let go of the idea that if you just tried harder, if you just loved more, if you just said the right thing, then maybe they would finally see your worth. But the truth is, **the right people won't need convincing to treat you well.**

So this is the last time you let them make you feel small. The last time you justify their lack of effort. The last time you accept less than what you know you deserve. You need to decide that your peace is more important than their presence. That your self-worth isn't up for negotiation. That loving someone doesn't mean you have to accept mistreatment, emotional inconsistency, or one-sided effort. Because the truth is, the moment you finally decide to walk away for real, you'll already know in your heart that you made the right decision. And that's when you'll realize—**this is the last time they'll ever make you feel this way.** Because after this, you'll never tolerate it again.

True closure isn't about getting an apology or an explanation—it's about making peace with the fact that you may never get one. It's about realizing that closure is a choice, not something some-

127

one else gives you. Not every insult needs a rebuttal. Not every misunderstanding needs an explanation. And more importantly, not every toxic situation needs your participation.

> *The peace you feel without their presence in your life, is worth being the villain in their story.*

Walking away is a powerful decision, but it comes with unexpected emotions. Even as you reclaim your worth and set firm boundaries, you may find yourself experiencing a surprising grief. This next chapter explores the complex emotions that arise when you choose growth, even when that growth means leaving parts of your old life behind.

CHAPTER 12

The Grief of Growth: Mourning Relationships Left Behind

No one tells you about the profound sadness that comes with outgrowing relationships. There's a special kind of sorrow that arrives not from losing what was taken from you, but from consciously choosing to walk away from connections that once felt like home. This isn't the same grief as losing someone suddenly. It's a gradual, often silent realization that your path is diverging from people who once walked alongside you.

You notice it in subtle moments—a conversation where you realize you're speaking a language they no longer understand. A shared experience that doesn't resonate the way it once did. A growing discomfort in social spaces that used to feel like your natural habitat. It's a strange kind of heartbreak—to love someone, to have shared years of laughter, support, and connection, yet to feel yourself slowly drifting toward a different horizon.

I don't walk away to teach people a lesson.
I walk away because I finally learned mine.

At first, you try to bridge the gap. You make excuses for the growing distance. You tell yourself nothing fundamental has changed in the relationship. But deep down, you know the truth: as you evolve, some connections can't evolve with you. And that recognition brings its own unique pain—the discomfort of sharing space with people who still expect a version of you that no longer exists.

But here's what you need to understand: **transformation is not betrayal**. Evolution is not abandonment. What feels like leaving others behind is often simply the courage to stop abandoning yourself. The reality is more nuanced than just "outgrowing" people, as though they're somehow less than you. Sometimes it's simply that your soul is called in a different direction. Some relationships are meant to be lifelong journeys; others are meant to be beautiful chapters in your story—with a beginning, middle, and end.

That doesn't diminish what you shared. That doesn't invalidate the love that was real. That doesn't require you to sever connections with harshness or indifference. It simply means accepting the natural evolution of human connection rather than forcing continuity where a natural completion has occurred.

What makes this transition harder isn't just guilt—it's the weight of shared history. When people have known you for years, they don't just know you; they've played a role in creating aspects of who you are. Walking away can feel like losing pieces of your own story, even when it's necessary for your growth. Some people will surprise you by celebrating your transformation, even when it means the relationship must change form. They'll love who you're becoming even more than who you were. They'll find joy in your growth even if you no longer fit neatly into the space they've held for you.

> *You don't always have to tell your*
> *side of the story... Time will.*

But others will resist—not always from bad intentions, but from their own fear of change and loss. They'll mistake your growth for rejection. They'll interpret your new boundaries as punishment. They'll try to convince you that loyalty means staying the same forever. But ask yourself this—what is the deeper betrayal? To acknowledge when a connection has run its natural course, or to live a half-life of compromise just to keep others comfortable? To honor what was by allowing it to take its place in your past, or to weaken its meaning by forcing it into a future where it no longer belongs?

You can honor people while still releasing your grip on relationships that have completed their purpose. You can be grateful for what they gave you without forcing them into a story they no longer fit. You can cherish the past without sacrificing your own evolution.

You don't need closure from others. You don't need permission to grow. You don't need to explain why you are choosing a life that finally feels like your own. Because deep down, you already know: relationships, like people, aren't meant to remain static. Some connections serve us for a season, others for a lifetime, but all are valid parts of our journey.

> *You can be friends with people for years and*
> *it can take years for you to realize*
> *they were never your friend.*

As you work through the grief of outgrown relationships and say goodbye to connections that no longer serve you, you enter a new phase. The external letting go now gives way to a deeper, internal transformation—one that requires facing the empty space that remains when familiar relationships and identities fall away.

CHAPTER 13

The Emergence of
Your Authentic Self

There is a **fire in you** that has been waiting to be unleashed. A power that has been buried under overthinking, self-doubt, guilt, and fear. You have spent so much of your life carrying things that were never meant for you—expectations, old wounds, the weight of people's opinions, the heaviness of a past that no longer fits who you are becoming. And now, it's time to witness the emergence of who you truly are. Completely. Unapologetically. Authentically.

Transformation isn't just about leaving behind what hurts you. It's about the beautiful unfolding of your true nature—the person you were always meant to become before life's circumstances taught you to hide parts of yourself. It's about discovering the gifts, strengths, and qualities that were always within you, waiting for the right conditions to flourish and be expressed.

The older I get, the less I feel the need to be included,
understood or accepted.

The butterfly's transformation offers the perfect example for this process. The caterpillar doesn't simply grow wings—it completely dissolves within its chrysalis, becoming neither what it was nor what it will be, but pure potential. Scientists call this the "imaginal stage," where total reorganization happens. In the same way, as you emerge from old patterns and relationships, you're not simply becoming a slightly different version of your former self. You're experiencing a fundamental rewiring of who you are at your core.

This is your time. The time to express the authentic voice you've silenced for too long. The time to honor your natural talents and abilities rather than the ones others expected of you. The time to live according to your true values, not the values imposed upon you. You owe no one an explanation for this authenticity. The only thing you owe yourself is permission to express who you've always been beneath all the adaptations and compromises.

The person emerging now isn't new—they've been within you all along. What's new is your willingness to let them be seen. *Your tendency to overthink is replaced by quiet confidence in your own instincts.* Your need for approval transforms into steady self-trust. The weight of guilt lifts as you recognize the inherent worthiness of your needs and boundaries.

This emergence is what being authentic truly means. It's not about creating a more appealing personality or becoming someone different. It's about removing the layers of protection and performance that covered your essential self. It's about returning to the wisdom and understanding you were born with, now enriched by your life experiences and lessons learned along the way.

Moving forward authentically means knowing your worth without needing external validation. It means trusting your perceptions without constant second-guessing. It means expressing your truth with the simple clarity of someone who no longer fears disapproval. It means choosing what genuinely nourishes your spirit rather than what pleases others.

You are not lost. You are not broken. **You are not someone who needs to be fixed.** You are someone who is finally allowing your true nature to emerge, free from others' expectations. And in this authentic expression lies your greatest power and strength.

So take this moment to recognize the emergence happening within you. Feel the power of living aligned with your truth. Know the peace that comes from no longer fighting against your own nature. And step forward—not as a new person, but as the real you who has been waiting all along to be expressed.

Just believe. Nobody has met you by accident.
God has planned everything.

The emergence of your authentic self is a profound journey, but living from this place requires consistent practice and practical choices. How do you maintain connection with your true nature when old patterns try to resurface? How do you navigate a world that may not be ready for the authentic you? The following approaches will help you anchor this emerging self in your daily life.

CHAPTER 14

The Empty Space: Death and Rebirth of Identity

Some roads you need to take alone.
No friends, no family, no partner. Just you and God.

Beyond the grief of outgrowing relationships and the emergence of your authentic self lies an even deeper challenge—**the empty space where your old identity dissolves completely**. This isn't just about changing your outer life or discovering new parts of yourself. It's about facing the void that appears when you step beyond who you've always thought you were.

This empty space isn't a detour on your path—it's where you need to go. After you've walked away from toxic relationships, left behind harmful patterns, and started speaking with your true voice, you reach a clearing. Here, you face not just the absence of others, but the fading of your familiar sense of self.

At first, this emptiness feels like relief. The weight of pretending lifts. The exhaustion of keeping up appearances fades. You can breathe without the pressure to be someone you're not. But then comes a different kind of discomfort—a *deep confusion* that few people talk about. You start to see how much of your identity was built around adaptations, defenses, and habits.

Those weekend drinking sessions you thought were "unwinding" were actually numbing. The social media scrolling you called "staying connected" was avoiding deeper connection with yourself. The overworking you labeled "ambition" was keeping you from facing what truly mattered. When these familiar anchors of identity fall away, you face the scary but freeing question: **Who am I without these patterns?**

> *That empty space in your bed is better than having a wrong person next to you.*

This void is where most people turn back—not because they want to, but because losing your sense of self creates a dizziness unlike anything else. Without the familiar landmarks of your old self, you temporarily lose your way. You might wonder: *Was I really that unhappy before? Maybe I should go back to my old ways. Maybe it's better to be someone I recognize than to face this emptiness.*

Your old self doesn't give up easily. Like someone being pushed out of their home, it will give you reasons why this journey into emptiness is foolish or dangerous. It will bring up memories of past failures as proof that you can't change. It will turn your doubts into loud warnings.

But this resistance isn't a sign you're going the wrong way— **it's proof you're getting close to a breakthrough**.

Think of this empty space like a cleared lot where an old building once stood. The old structure is gone, creating a temporary emptiness that might look like nothing to someone passing by. But the builder sees something different—the perfect spot for something new to be created. Without this clearing, nothing new could be built.

Unlike earlier parts of your journey where you could see progress through outer changes or emotional shifts, **this phase often looks invisible to others and feels hard to explain even to yourself**. You won't necessarily feel "better" in obvious ways. Instead, you'll notice subtle shifts:

- You'll see thoughts and feelings as passing events rather than who you are
- You'll find yourself less triggered by things that once sent you spiraling
- You'll notice a small pause between what happens and how you respond
- You'll feel less need to defend positions or identities you once clung to

This is the shift from being your thoughts to watching your thoughts happen. From being your emotions to observing them come and go. It's moving from being caught in your story to watching the story unfold.

The self you're outgrowing served important purposes. It helped you navigate childhood wounds, survive difficult times, and create enough stability to function in the world. **This old self wasn't a mistake—it was a necessary shell that protected you until now.** Thank it for its service instead of judging it.

What makes this phase different is that you're not just trading one identity for another—you're discovering the awareness that exists beyond all identities. This isn't about becoming a "better version" of yourself. It's about recognizing that your deepest nature exists beyond all versions, all self-images, all constructed identities.

> *There were things you said years ago that you no longer agree with today. There were things you did years ago that you don't do anymore. No, you are not two faced, you are simply growing and changing as you should be. As we all should be.*

The surprising truth about this empty space is that what feels like losing yourself actually reveals what can never be lost. The real you isn't another identity—it's the awareness that remains when all identities fall away. What you feared losing was never actually who you were. Your essence was always the consciousness watching the show, not the character you were playing. As you get comfortable with this spaciousness, something amazing happens. The emptiness you feared wasn't empty at all—it was full of possibilities that couldn't grow while you were holding tight to your old self. This apparent void contains everything you need to create authentically.

In the space beyond who you thought you were, you discover who you've always been. Not as a fixed identity, but as the open awareness from which all experiences arise—the canvas on which all self-images are temporarily painted but which itself remains untouched. When you no longer need to defend a particular idea of yourself, you're free to respond to life with flexibility and realness. When you're not trapped by who you believe you should be, you can express who you actually are in each moment—not as an act but as a natural unfolding.

This is the greatest freedom—not freedom to become whatever you want, but freedom from the belief that you need to become anything at all to be worthy of existence. The empty space isn't the end of your journey. It's the clearing from which your authentic life begins to grow—no longer limited by who you once believed yourself to be.

PART 4

Solutions

*Funny thing about getting older...your eyesight may
weaken yet you can see through people much better.*

You've reached the point where awareness crystallizes into action. The fog of doubt has lifted, revealing what you've perhaps known all along: some dynamics can't be fixed, some people won't change, and sometimes the only path forward is to walk away. But how do you trust this knowing when manipulation has made you question your own reality? How do you find the courage to leave when guilt still tugs at your conscience? How do you navigate the grief of outgrowing relationships and identities that once defined you?

The first step toward freedom from manipulation is rebuilding trust in your own perception. When someone has consistently made you doubt yourself, you need concrete strategies to reestablish connection with reality. The following approach helps you reclaim your internal compass without getting drawn back into exhausting debates about what is or isn't true.

When someone has systematically undermined your confidence in your own perceptions, rebuilding that trust becomes your first priority. The most effective approach isn't trying to convince the manipulator of your reality—it's strengthening your own connection to it.

REALITY ANCHORING: RECLAIMING YOUR PERCEPTION

God will expose every person in your life
who is NOT for you. You won't have to dig...
the proof will fall right into your lap.

Implement the **Reality Preservation Protocol** to counteract gaslighting and manipulation:

First, create an objective record. In a private journal (preferably digital and password-protected), document specific interactions immediately after they occur. Include exact quotes, contextual details, and your unfiltered emotional response. This isn't paranoia—it's protection against the memory distortion that manipulation creates. Research on memory formation shows that each time we recall an event, we actually reconstruct it rather than retrieving an intact record. Without documentation, repeated challenges to your perception can literally rewrite your memories.

Next, selectively share your experience with a trusted outsider—someone who has no connection to the manipulator and no stake in your shared dynamics. Simply describe what happened without editorializing, then ask: "Does this seem reasonable to you?" This external validation isn't about gathering allies but about calibrating your reality meter when manipulation has tampered with its settings.

Finally, recognize manipulation tactics in real time with these identification questions:

- "Am I feeling confused about something that should be straightforward?"
- "Do I find myself constantly explaining or defending basic perceptions?"
- "Do I feel worse about myself after interactions with this person?"
- "Is there a pattern of my concerns being turned back on me?"

When you notice these signs, implement an immediate **Cognitive Protection Response**:

1. Pause the conversation: "I need to think about this more clearly."
2. Physically step back or create literal distance.
3. Mentally affirm: "My perceptions are valid even if challenged."
4. Decline to engage in debates about what you experienced.

This approach is particularly effective because it sidesteps the trap of trying to convince manipulators, who are invested in maintaining their alternative reality. Instead, it focuses on preserving your connection to truth—the foundation of all authentic decision-making.

> *I saved some people's reputation by not telling*
> *my side of the story. It's best to stay silent through*
> *the storms. Toxic people usually destroy themselves*
> *in the process of trying to destroy you.*

Once you've strengthened your connection to reality, you face the challenge of actually leaving—not just physically, but emotionally and psychologically. Many people struggle with multiple "false exits" before making a clean break. These strategies help you move beyond the cycle of "one more chance" to make a departure that truly lasts.

THE DEFINITIVE DEPARTURE: BEYOND "ONE MORE CHANCE"

> *I don't care what anyone says...*
> *Good people get tired of being good to ungrateful people.*

The most difficult threshold to cross isn't deciding to leave but actually leaving. After multiple false starts, postponed departures, and "final" chances, how do you make this time truly different?

The answer lies in understanding what is referred to as the "extinction burst"—the temporary intensification of unwanted behavior when reinforcement is withdrawn. This explains why, when you've previously tried to leave, manipulative people suddenly improve just enough to keep you attached, only to revert once security is restored.

Break this cycle with the **Clean Break Protocol**:

First, crystallize your decision through the **Point of No Return Exercise**. List every promise that's been broken, every pattern that's repeated, every hopeful expectation that's been disappointed. Be ruthlessly specific. Then answer one question: "If this exact pattern continues for five more years, am I willing to live with it?" This question cuts through the hope of change and focuses on the reality of consistency.

Once your decision is clear, create a **Departure Plan** with these elements:

- Practical logistics (financial arrangements, living situations, shared possessions)
- Support resources (people who will sustain you through difficult moments)
- Anticipated manipulation tactics (how they'll likely respond and your prepared counters)
- Non-negotiable boundaries for any final communication

When implementing your departure, embrace the **Communication Minimalism Principle**:

- Use direct, unambiguous language

- Avoid explaining your reasoning (which only creates openings for debate)
- Decline negotiations, suggested compromises, or promises of change
- Communicate once and completely, then disengage

What makes this approach powerful is its recognition that the urge to explain comes from lingering guilt, not practical necessity. As therapist Shannon Thomas notes in her research on psychological abuse, "Closure is something you give yourself, not something you get from someone else."

> *You know what I would really like to see go viral?*
> *Basic human decency.*

After leaving behind relationships and patterns that defined you, you enter the disorienting space between who you were and who you're becoming. This transitional territory can be frightening, but with the right framework, you can move through it with greater ease and purpose.

NAVIGATING IDENTITY TRANSITION

The space between who you were and who you're becoming is perhaps the most challenging territory to traverse. You've left behind relationships, patterns, and identities that, however limiting, provided a sense of familiarity. Now you face "identity discontinuity"—the disorienting sense that you are no longer the same person, yet not fully formed into some-one new.

*You should be flattered. There was a group effort
to take you down and you are still standing.*

Move through this terrain with the **Identity Bridge Framework**:

First, honor the self you're leaving behind. This constructed identity, with all its limitations, served a vital purpose—it protected you when you needed protection. Create a private ritual acknowledging both its service and its completion. Write a letter to this former self, expressing gratitude for its survival strategies while gently explaining why those strategies are no longer needed.

Next, navigate the void between identities by creating **Transitional Anchors**—small, concrete practices that provide stability while you transform:

- Daily rituals that ground you in sensation rather than thought
- Creative expression without judgment or purpose
- Connection with nature, which transcends human identity constructs
- Movement practices that relocate awareness from mind to body

These anchors aren't distractions from the discomfort of transition—they're stable reference points as you move through it. Research on major life transitions shows that maintaining certain constants during periods of change significantly reduces associated psychological distress.

Finally, practice **Emergent Identity Cultivation**—actively nurturing the self that's being born:

- Experiment with new responses to old triggers
- Notice when you naturally act in ways that surprise the old self
- Deliberately practice unfamiliar behaviors that align with your deeper values
- Celebrate moments of authenticity even when they feel foreign or uncomfortable

What makes this approach unique is its recognition that identity transformation isn't about rejection but evolution. You're not becoming someone different—you're becoming more authentically who you've always been beneath adaptive patterns that once served but now constrain you.

The final challenge isn't about techniques but about finding the courage to walk a path that may have no external validation. When you've been conditioned to seek approval or certainty, this requires developing a new relationship with the unknown and learning to trust your own internal guidance system.

THE COURAGE OF UNCHARTED TERRITORY

The final stage of liberation isn't about techniques or strategies—it's about embracing the fundamental courage of walking your own path, even when that path isn't fully visible, even when there's no external validation confirming you're headed in the right direction.

Cultivate this courage through the **Uncertainty Embrace Practice**:

Each day, deliberately do one thing for which you have no script, no precedent in your history, no guarantee of success. Start small—express a preference you would typically silence, create a boundary you would normally abandon, pursue an interest your former self would have dismissed. With each step into the unknown, you strengthen your tolerance for uncertainty—the essential skill for authentic living.

When doubt inevitably arises, implement the **Soul Compass Check**:

1. Place your hand on your heart or solar plexus
2. Ask yourself: "Does this choice create expansion or contraction in my being?"
3. Notice the physical sensation that arises—a subtle opening or tightening
4. Trust this body-wisdom over intellectual justifications

This practice taps into what neuroscientists call interoception—your brain's perception of your body's internal state—

which research increasingly shows plays a crucial role in intuitive decision-making. By learning to detect subtle physical cues that precede conscious thought, you access wisdom that manipulation cannot touch.

Reinforce your courage daily with the **Freedom Affirmation**—not as empty positive thinking but as an active declaration of sovereignty: "I am the author of my life. I trust my perception. I honor my needs. I walk away from what diminishes me. I move toward what enlarges me. I owe no explanation for my evolution."

THE INTEGRATION

> *You will always win when you move with*
> *love and genuine intentions. Always.*

The journey from manipulation to liberation, from self-doubt to self-trust, from confinement to courage isn't a single decision but a daily practice of choosing yourself. It begins with anchoring your reality against gaslighting and manipulation. It continues with making a definitive departure from cycles that diminish you. It deepens as you navigate the disorienting but necessary transformation of identity. And it culminates in the courage to walk an uncharted path guided by your own internal compass.

This isn't just about specific relationships or situations you're leaving behind. It's about permanently altering how you move through the world—with clarity, conviction, and an unwavering commitment to your own experience. It's about recognizing that your perspective matters, your needs matter, your authentic expression matters—not because someone else validates these things, but because you do.

The fire that's been waiting to be unleashed isn't something you need to create. It's something you simply need to stop suppressing. It's been there all along, beneath the doubt, beneath the guilt, beneath the fear. And now, as you step fully into your own authority, it illuminates not just your path, but the very reason you were born—to express a truth that only you can embody, to offer a gift that only you can give.

> *Betrayal is the ultimate act of cowardice.*
> *It takes courage to be honest, but it takes no courage*
> *to deceive. It is a choice, not a mistake. It's a conscious*
> *decision to put self interest above loyalty and truth.*

With these practical strategies for liberation in hand, we can now explore even deeper dimensions of transformation. The tools we've covered so far address the symptoms and immediate causes of emotional reactivity, but lasting freedom requires understanding the more subtle patterns operating beneath the surface—the hidden mechanisms that keep us trapped even when we're actively trying to change.

PART 5

BEYOND THE SURFACE – THE DIFFERENT IDEAS THAT ARE JUST AS IMPORTANT

CHAPTER 15

You Can Do It

People showed me their true colors this year.
I needed that.

How many times have you actually progressed without realizing it? How many times have you overcome something, big or small, that once felt impossible? I remember the first time I ever went snowboarding. It was actually the first time I had ever seen snow. I was 16 years old and went away with my brother, sister and their partners. My brother had been before so told me to go to a group lesson where they teach you. All I can say is...I left that day and thought to myself, "I will never get this!" I fell so many times, I had bruises. I thought it was the hardest thing I'd ever done. I was literally stuck to a board in the most unnatural position I'd ever been in. I told my brother I was just going to relax for the rest of the trip, but he convinced me that if I keep going, I'll get it.

The next day, I went to the group lesson again...and guess what? I got a little better. My confidence started to build. By the fourth day I was going down the slope on my own. Still falling at times, but considerably better and having a lot of fun. This is the thing...Your mind is wired to focus on what hasn't changed yet and what you cannot do, but if you looked at yourself from the outside, you'd see how far you've already come. **The problem isn't that you're stuck—it's that your thoughts convince you that you are.**

The truth is, you're never actually stuck. You always have choices. They might not be easy choices, and they might come with risk, but they exist. The real reason you feel stuck isn't because you can't move forward—but because you're afraid to. Maybe you're afraid of failing. Maybe you're afraid of what people will think if you take a risk and fall flat on your face. Maybe you're afraid that even if you try, nothing will change. And so, instead of confronting that fear, you choose inaction. You convince yourself that you're powerless, even when you're not.

Part of what makes us feel stuck is the stagnant energy that comes from repetition. Day after day, doing the same things in the same places, your energy gets trapped in familiar patterns. Think about it—how many times have you felt reinvigorated just by changing your environment? Taking a walk, traveling somewhere new, even just rearranging your furniture. There's a reason for that. **Movement creates new energy. New spaces create new possibilities.**

I remember when I was caught in an exhausting cycle of anxiety and rumination. For weeks, I tried to mentally power through it. I kept telling myself I needed to be stronger, that I should be able to fix my thought patterns through sheer willpower. I meditated, journaled, and practiced all the mental techniques I knew, yet the anxious thoughts continued to loop endlessly. And even though all of that helped momentarily, little did I realize there was another underlying repetitive energy that was building...and I had to address it.

It wasn't until I decided to go away on a road trip that everything changed. About two hours into the drive, something remarkable happened—I started to feel my anxiety and looping thoughts dissolve. I hadn't developed better coping skills in those two hours; I had simply changed my physical location. The further I drove from my familiar environment, the quieter my mind became. Sometimes what we interpret as a mental block is actually an environmental one.

This is why sometimes the most powerful step you can take isn't doubling down on mental effort but simply changing your surroundings. A weekend away, a day spent in nature, even working from a different location can create the mental space needed for new perspectives to emerge. Physical distance often translates to psychological distance, allowing you to see your situation through fresh eyes.

When energy becomes stagnant, your thoughts start to loop. The same worries, the same fears, the same self-doubts play on repeat in your mind. And because nothing in your environment is changing, nothing in your internal landscape changes either. You're looking at the same problems from the same perspective, so of course, you're coming up with the same solutions—or lack thereof.

Growth doesn't come from waiting for the perfect moment. It comes from deciding that where you are is no longer an option. It comes from taking action even when you're scared, even when you don't feel "ready," even when the outcome is uncertain. Sometimes that action might be as simple as putting yourself in a new environment, especially in nature, where the constant background noise of your anxious thoughts can finally quiet down.

And if you feel like you're stuck, ask yourself this: *Am I actually stuck, or am I just scared to do something different?* Or perhaps: *Have I been in the same environment too long, trying to solve problems with the same mind that created them?* Because more often than not, the only thing keeping you in place isn't the world around you—it's the story in your mind. And the moment you decide to move, whether that's taking a different action or simply changing your physical location, you'll realize you've been capable of progress all along. But what creates these limiting stories in the first place? Behind these mental barriers lies a powerful force that both protects and constrains you—the ego. Understanding how this silent trickster operates is the key to liberating yourself from the illusion of stagnation.

CHAPTER 16

The Ego's Silent Trickery:
How Your Mind Keeps
You Small

*Sometimes people will act like you're hard to
deal with because you aren't easy to fool.*

Ego is often misunderstood. It's easy to think of it as arrogance, the person who brags loudly, takes up space, and believes they are superior to everyone else. **But ego is much quieter than that.** It doesn't just show up as overconfidence—it also appears as self-doubt, fear of judgment, and hesitation to put yourself out there.

Ego is what stops you from sharing your thoughts because you're afraid people will disagree. Ego is what makes you second-guess your dreams because failing would feel humiliating. Ego is the voice that convinces you to stay in your comfort zone, telling you that playing it safe is better than taking a risk. Ego tells you that you are always right, and doesn't want you to learn, change or grow. Ego wants you to remain stuck, creating the same cycles.

But here's the trap: **The ego's number one goal isn't to make you happy—it's to keep you safe.** And in doing so, it often keeps you small. It makes you hesitate before stepping into the unknown, clinging to an illusion of control that doesn't actually exist. It convinces you that if you just avoid embarrassment, rejection, or failure, you'll be fine. But has avoiding these things ever truly made you feel better? Has shrinking yourself to avoid risk ever led to real confidence?

The biggest trick your ego plays is making you believe that if you avoid discomfort, you will be protected. But in reality, avoiding discomfort only makes it worse. **You don't gain confidence by playing it safe—you gain confidence by proving to yourself that you can handle whatever comes your way.**

Think about the things you've avoided because of ego. How many times have you held back from expressing yourself because you feared judgment? How many times have you turned down an opportunity because failing at it would feel worse than never trying at all? The ego would rather let you live with the regret of not trying than with the temporary sting of trying and failing. But in the long run, which one hurts more?

The truth is, the ego is just another mental construct. It's a defense mechanism built from your past experiences, social conditioning, and personal fears. But it is not you. The moment you recognize its tricks, you gain power over it. You stop letting fear make your decisions. You stop avoiding opportunities because of what people might think. You stop letting an illusion of safety keep you from experiencing real growth. Your ego will always try to protect you. But it's up to you to decide whether you want to live a protected life or a fulfilled one.

If you get a different ME,
that means I saw the REAL you.

As we move beyond the ways our ego can limit us, we encounter one of life's most complex topics: forgiveness in order to heal. We've all heard different perspectives on forgiveness—from spiritual traditions to self-help books to personal advice. But healing rarely follows a straight line, and our relationship with forgiveness can be deeply personal. What does forgiveness truly mean? Is there only one way to find peace after being wounded? In exploring these questions, we might discover that healing contains more nuance than we've been led to believe, and that finding our own authentic path forward might look different than we expected.

PART 6

WAYS TO FREEDOM

CHAPTER 17

What They Didn't Tell You About Forgiveness

Throughout our lives, we encounter the teaching that forgiveness is essential for healing. The message seems clear: to find peace, we must forgive those who have harmed us. Yet as we delve deeper into the journey of healing, we discover a more nuanced truth—one that honors both the profound power of forgiveness and the deeply personal nature of each person's healing path.

When someone has fundamentally altered how you see yourself, how you move through the world, or how safe you feel in your own body, the question of forgiveness becomes more complex than inspirational quotes might suggest. These profound wounds touch the very core of our being, reshaping our relationship with ourselves and with the world around us.

In these situations, healing doesn't always follow a prescribed formula. Sometimes, the path to wholeness involves acknowledging that certain wounds need to be honored differently. This isn't about harboring vengeance or remaining bitter— it's about recognizing that true healing comes from authenticity, not from forcing yourself to forgive before you're genuinely ready.

There can be quiet strength in choosing to prioritize your own healing over premature forgiveness. This choice reflects clarity, not resentment—a clear-eyed acceptance of what happened and a commitment to your own wellbeing. You've acknowledged the reality without diminishing it. You've accepted that the other person may never change, apologize, or take responsibility. And you've found peace through boundaries and self-respect rather than through forgiveness that doesn't yet feel authentic.

Consider your body's natural healing process. When you suffer a deep cut, your body doesn't **need** to "forgive" what cut it in order to heal. It requires proper care—cleaning the wound, protecting it from further harm, giving it time, and perhaps medical attention. The body's wisdom lies in prioritizing restoration rather than reconciliation with the object that caused the injury. Our emotional healing can follow a similar pattern—focusing first on our own recovery rather than on our relationship with what harmed us, regardless of how long that takes.

True forgiveness, when it arises naturally from within, holds tremendous power, and I guess is the pinnacle we'd all like to get to one day, for every situation. But only when, or if, we are ever ready. When it emerges as a genuine release that feels right for you—not from external pressure or obligation—it can be profoundly liberating. Yet this kind of forgiveness cannot be manufactured or rushed. It arrives in its own time, like a flower that blooms when conditions are right, not when we demand it.

What many don't openly discuss is how forgiveness pursued from a sense of obligation rather than genuine readiness can actually impede healing. Those who force themselves to forgive prematurely often find themselves caught in cycles of continued harm or lingering resentment that they then feel guilty about. The dissonance between what they believe they should feel and what they actually feel creates additional suffering—now they're not only processing the original wound but also feeling inadequate for not forgiving "properly."

Your relationship with forgiveness may evolve over time. What feels impossible today might gradually transform as you rebuild yourself. Perhaps one day, when the wound no longer defines any part of your identity, forgiveness may arrive unexpectedly—not because the other person deserves it, but because you no longer need to withhold it to protect yourself. Or perhaps your path leads elsewhere—and that, too, is perfectly valid.

The essence of healing isn't about meeting external expectations but about becoming whole again. It's about reclaiming your authentic self, not performing forgiveness to appear virtuous or "healed" by others' standards. You need not justify your healing journey to anyone. You're allowed to define your own path forward:

I honor my own timeline for healing. I release the pressure to feel compassion before I'm ready. I recognize there are many paths to freedom.

What truly matters isn't whether you forgive, but whether you're able to move forward with your life in a way that feels authentic and whole. Many people have built rich, fulfilling lives defined by their own values without ever reaching the point of forgiveness for certain deep wounds—and this hasn't made their healing any less complete. They've found ways to process their experiences, integrate the lessons, establish clear boundaries, and redirect their energy toward what brings them joy and purpose.

There's a profound difference between being stuck in bitterness and consciously choosing not to forgive while still moving forward. The former keeps you tethered to the past, while the latter acknowledges what happened without allowing it to determine your future. You can release the stranglehold that someone had on your life without necessarily offering them forgiveness. You can stop carrying the weight of their actions without absolution. You can reclaim your power and your peace without completing the particular ritual of forgiveness that society often demands.

When you reclaim this sovereignty over your healing journey, something remarkable happens. You begin to touch something deeper than the stories of what happened to you—a fundamental wellspring of inner peace that exists beyond any particular relationship or past wound. This shift moves your focus from external circumstances to the cultivation of your own internal harmony.

While forgiveness concerns how we relate to others and our past, inner peace addresses how we relate to ourselves in the present moment. And ultimately, this relationship with yourself may be the most profound healing of all.

CHAPTER 18

Beyond Happiness: Finding Inner Peace

You cannot fix someone who doesn't want to be fixed,
but you can ruin your life trying.

You're human...that's it. Just allow yourself to be human and not perfect. Here's a truth that might be hard to swallow: happiness, as we've been taught to understand it, is largely a myth. The pursuit of constant happiness is perhaps the most misguided quest we undertake. It's also a relatively new obsession in human history—this idea that we should be in a perpetual state of joy and satisfaction.

Think about it: when did we decide that being happy all the time was the goal of human existence? And what is happening anyway? What warrants that term? Is it going out and having fun, is it being on a high, is it always being at peace and never having any issues? When did we start believing something was wrong with us if we weren't constantly feeling "good"?

This modern myth of happiness has set us up for profound disappointment. We've been sold the idea that if we just find the right job, partner, house, body, or lifestyle, we'll unlock some state of permanent contentment. But this promise is fundamentally flawed.

Happiness, by its very nature, is fleeting. It comes and goes. It rises and falls with circumstances, with hormones, with weather, with the countless variables of life that are beyond our control. The more desperately we chase it, the more it seems to evade us. The more we try to hold onto happy moments, the quicker they slip through our fingers. And in constantly pursuing this elusive state, we miss the richness of the full human experience.

Part of accepting our humanity is acknowledging that **we're always in the process of learning**—and that process rarely follows a straight line. Sometimes we make the same mistake for fifteen years. We circle back to the same kinds of people who hurt us before. We return to self-destructive habits we swore we'd never do again. We find ourselves in patterns so familiar that we can predict their painful endings before they even begin.

But what about the smaller mistakes we make daily? The missed opportunity, the careless word, the forgotten task? We're often far harsher on ourselves for these everyday missteps than for our larger patterns. *There is liberation in saying "I made a mistake and it's ok,"* and then moving forward without dwelling. It's when you try to resist and attempt to correct what's already happened that anxiety creeps in. You have to give yourself room to be imperfect. The more you understand that making mistakes is simply part of being human, the less power they have over you.

When you make a small mistake, feel it fully for a moment, then allow yourself to move on by accepting it. You'll quickly realize it's rarely the end of the world. Life constantly presents new opportunities if you keep moving forward instead of looking back. That meeting where you misspoke? That email with the typo? That moment of forgetfulness? Stop replaying these moments. Accept them, give yourself grace to be human, and you'll have discovered a key to daily peace.

It's easy to look back and think: *I should have known better. I've wasted so much time. Why did it take me so long to see what was right in front of me?* But the truth is both simpler and more profound: if you really knew—if you truly, deeply knew at your core—you would have made the decision you're making now. You only know what you know at any point in your life, and you make changes when you are genuinely ready. If you didn't change sooner, it simply means you still had more to learn.

This is why the timing of change is often more perfect than we realize. The lessons we need to learn don't arrive when we think they should—they arrive when we're finally prepared to receive them. That relationship you stayed in too long? Those years repeating the same patterns? **They weren't wasted time.** They were the exact experience you needed to bring you to this moment of clarity. To this precise point of transformation. This is your journey, as unique as your fingerprint...no one else's.

Look at nature—nothing in the natural world exists in a constant state. There are seasons, cycles, ebbs and flows. Trees don't bloom year-round. Animals don't migrate continuously. The ocean doesn't maintain a single tide. So why do we expect our emotional lives to be any different? Why have we pathologized normal human emotions like sadness, anger, frustration, or grief by labeling them as obstacles to this mythical state of perpetual happiness?

What if, instead of chasing happiness, we sought something deeper? Something more sustainable? What if the goal isn't happiness at all, but understanding? **A state of being that doesn't depend on everything going right, but on your ability to comprehend and accept life even when things go wrong.** A fundamental recognition that life will contain joy and sorrow, ease and struggle, comfort and pain—and that all of these experiences have meaning.

The fear of change, the comfort of familiar pain, the ego's silent trickery—all of these are obstacles on the path to understanding. They keep us stuck in patterns that may feel safe but ultimately rob us of the fullness of life. Breaking free from these patterns isn't about reaching some state of perfect happiness. **It's about allowing yourself to be fully human**, with all the messiness and imperfection that entails and still giving yourself space to learn and evolve.

True understanding comes from acceptance—not resignation, but genuine recognition of what is. It comes from letting go of the constant struggle against reality and instead learning to work with it. It comes from releasing the need to control everything and everyone around you. It comes from trusting that you can comprehend whatever life brings, even if it's not what you expected or wanted.

This doesn't mean you never feel sad, angry, disappointed, or afraid. It means you don't resist these emotions or get caught in them. You allow them to move through you, teaching you what they came to teach, and then you let them go. You recognize that emotions, like thoughts, are temporary visitors, not permanent residents. In the quiet moments when you're not running from pain or chasing pleasure, when you're simply present with what is, you'll find that understanding was never really lost. It was just waiting for you to stop long enough to notice it. And in that noticing, in that returning to yourself, you'll discover that what you've been searching for has been with you all along.

So maybe the question isn't "How can I be happy?" but rather **"How can I understand and accept what is?"** Because when you find that understanding, happiness no longer needs to be chased. It becomes simply another color in the rich tapestry of a life fully lived.

When we release the exhausting pursuit of constant happiness and embrace deep understanding instead, something remarkable begins to happen. The acceptance of life's full spectrum—

its joys and sorrows, its comforts and challenges—creates space for a deeper dimension of experience to emerge. And in that very understanding, is where true appreciation for life exists. There is a quietness, a peace in understanding life's ups and downs, that nothing else can give.

PART 7

THE LIGHT

CHAPTER 19

Finding Light in Life's Journey

As we first visited in the book, there's something about those first moments of waking that can feel so heavy. I know this intimately—that space between sleep and consciousness when yesterday's worries and tomorrow's uncertainties rush in all at once. Most mornings, I wake with that weight pressing against my chest, a vague sense of unease that arrives before I've even opened my eyes. Sometimes it's just a feeling of negativity that I can't really explain or understand at the time, I just feel it. But, there is light.

I do my best to never leave the house carrying that heaviness. This is where my journey begins each day—not in denying the weight, but in choosing what else I will carry alongside it. With my hand placed gently over my heart, I whisper the words that have become my anchor: **"Thank you, for another day of life."** In that moment, it's the beginning of the shift. The day ahead might not be perfect—there might be challenges, disappointments, moments of frustration—but in this sacred morning ritual, I lay the foundation for how I'll meet whatever comes. I say to myself, "I am also in control of how I feel." Even if it's a small amount of control, it's something. I fill my heart with love and light, breath by breath, allowing gratitude to create space within me for both the reality of what is and the possibility of what could be.

This isn't about forcing positivity or pretending difficulties don't exist. It's about recognizing the profound gift of being alive for another day, of having another chance to love, to grow, to experience the extraordinary miracle of existence. When we truly understand that each day is not guaranteed but graciously given, everything changes. The ordinary becomes sacred. Small joys become treasures.

And in this space of appreciation, we begin to see with new eyes the incredible abundance that surrounds us, even in our most challenging seasons. The faces of those we love—family members and friends who know us fully and choose us anyway. *I visualize them in these quiet morning moments, letting my heart fill with gratitude for each unique soul journeying alongside me.* We get only one life with these particular people we love. One chance to fully appreciate the parent who sacrificed for us, the child whose growth we witness day by day, the friend who shows up consistently through life's storms, the partner who stands by us, the pet who is unconditionally loving or the most important of all, ourselves. I give thanks to myself.

Remember this... Your normal day is someone's dream.
So be thankful, every single day.

What began in those still moments before leaving my house has gradually expanded into a way of moving through the world. I've discovered that gratitude isn't just a feeling that comes and goes—it's a lens through which we can choose to view everything. When we look through this lens, we notice the small miracles we might otherwise miss—the warmth of sunlight across the floor, the melody of birds outside our window, the strength in a body that continues to carry us despite its imperfections.

I've come to believe deeply that everything good we put into the world returns to us multiplied. When we approach life with genuine thankfulness, we become more generous, more compassionate, more present. We become less affected by other peoples short comings. And these qualities inevitably attract similar energies back to us. Not just because we're manipulating some cosmic reward system, but because **appreciation fundamentally changes who we are and how we interact with the world**.

The most challenging periods of my life have revealed this truth most clearly. Looking back, I can see with perfect clarity how each apparent setback was actually setting me up for growth I couldn't yet imagine. It's true, our life has it's seasons, just like the weather. That relationship that ended painfully created space for deeper love to enter. That professional disappointment redirected me toward work that nourishes my soul.

That period of uncertainty taught me to trust life's unfolding in ways I never could have learned through ease alone.

And here's another truth I've discovered along the way: **we have enough time**. Despite our constant feeling of rushing, of time slipping away, we have enough time to pursue new dreams, new experiences, to succeed, to transform. Think of Nelson Mandela, who spent 27 years in prison. Twenty-seven years! Take a moment to reflect on where you were 27 years ago—that entire span of time, all those moments and experiences you've lived through since then, he spent in a cell. Unable to do all the things you've been free to do.

Consider this: Mandela was 71 years old when he was finally released from prison. At 75—an age when many believe life's most productive years are behind them—he became the president of South Africa. He emerged to transform a nation and leave a legacy that will echo through generations. Now I ask you: *What will you do with the next 27 years of your life?* What dreams might you fulfill, what impact might you have, what joy might you create with that same span of time?

If Mandela could achieve what he did after losing nearly three decades of his life, what might be possible for you? What dreams have you deferred, thinking "it's too late" or "I don't have enough time"? *The truth is that it's never too late to begin, to create, to transform, to live.* Everything happens for a reason— not in some predetermined sense where suffering is assigned to teach us lessons, but in the way that each experience shapes us into exactly who we need to become.

Through every storm, every heartbreak, every moment when I thought I couldn't possibly go on—life has proven that everything really does work out. Not always in the ways I expected. Not always on my timeline. But always in ways that ultimately served my growth and awakening. This isn't blind optimism; it's a truth I've witnessed again and again, both in my life and in the lives of countless others who have chosen to trust the journey even when the path ahead was shrouded in fog.

You've been on your own journey through these pages. You've faced truths about yourself that weren't always comfortable. You've recognized patterns that no longer serve you. You've begun the process of reclaiming parts of yourself that got lost along the way. And perhaps, like me, you still wake up some mornings feeling the weight of it all.

But I hope you also feel something else stirring within you—a quiet certainty that you are **exactly where you're meant to be**. Every challenge, every joy, every seemingly random encounter is weaving the unique tapestry of your life with exquisite precision. Nothing is wasted. Nothing is accidental. You are being shaped, moment by moment, into the person you're destined to become.

So tomorrow morning, when consciousness first returns and with it perhaps that familiar heaviness, place your hand on your heart. Feel whatever is there—the weight, the worry, the weariness. And then, breath by breath, fill that space with light and love as you whisper, "Thank you, for another day of life." Name the possibilities you're grateful for. Let appreciation wash through you, transforming how you'll meet this one precious day.

And as this book draws closer to the end, I give you this parting message... Every challenge is shaping you. Every joy is revealing you. Every moment is an opportunity to choose appreciation over resentment, gratitude over entitlement, presence over distraction. And in that choice—made again and again, morning after morning—lies a power greater than any obstacle you'll ever face. The power to see your one wild, and precious life, as the extraordinary gift it truly is. You're stronger than you think sometimes...you always have been.

CHAPTER 20

Go And Live

This is your chapter to write. Go and live...You've got this.

Love and Light,
Daniel Chidiac

I would just like to say...well done on completing this book. I mean that! It says a lot about your determination to improve yourself, which in itself speaks volumes about your character. And thank you, for giving me the opportunity to share this journey with you. I wish you all the best on your journey, and remember that you can always revisit what we've covered—whether it's a specific part or the entire book—until it truly sinks in. We all need a healthy reminder sometimes.

If you enjoyed this book and felt like it resonated with you, I'd really appreciate it if you left a short review. You can do so by scanning the QR code below:

Instagram: @danielchidiac
Tiktok: @daniel_chidiac
Facebook: @danielgchidiac